ST. JOSEPH
AND HIS
WORLD

ST. JOSEPH AND HIS WORLD

MIKE AQUILINA

with a foreword by Scott Hahn

 Scepter

Published by Scepter Publishers, Inc.
info@scepterpublishers.org
www.scepterpublishers.org
800-322-8773
New York
All rights reserved.

Cover art: Georges de La Tour, St. Joseph the Carpenter, 1640s. The Picture Art Collection / Alamy Stock Photo.
Cover design: by Studio Red Design
Text design and pagination: by Studio Red Design

Library of Congress Control Number: 2020944261

ISBN
Paperback: 9781594173936
eBook: 9781594173943

Printed in the United States of America

CONTENTS

For Benedetto

FOREWORD

By Scott Hahn

In the second century, the Greek historian Plutarch wrote his *Parallel Lives*, a collection of biographical profiles organized in pairs. Each pair consisted of one eminent Greek and one eminent Roman. It was a convenient format, enabling its author to enhance each profile with implicit comparisons to its complement: Alexander the Great with Julius Caesar, Demosthenes with Cicero, and so on. Plutarch wrote forty-eight biographies, all told.

In writing these biographies, he had the distinct advantage of writing as a pagan historian for a pagan audience. And why should that be an advantage? Because no one was expecting Plutarch to write a biography of St. Joseph.

There are few subjects so challenging, especially for authors who respect historical method. St. Joseph seems to go out of his way to be uncooperative with history, even as he's faithful to

Providence. In all the reliable records, he is as tight-lipped as an NSA agent, as unforthcoming as a Carthusian. Christian authors down through the ages have tended to make up for the dearth of information by supplying an excess of pious homiletics. At the end of such books, Joseph can seem more distant than he was on page one.

Faced with this challenge, Mike Aquilina succeeded by doubling the difficulty. Though he never shows his hand, he has, in the pages of *St. Joseph and His World*, pulled a Plutarch on us. He has composed "parallel lives" of the most improbable pair. He tells the story of the Holy Family's patriarch along-side the life of the man's arch-nemesis. He gives an account of Joseph's days as they were bound up with the career of one of history's vilest despots: King Herod the Great.

And this is a tremendous breakthrough, because we cannot begin to understand the life of either until we appreciate the life of the other.

We may not *want* to spend time reading about King Herod's astonishing depravity, but apart from it we cannot truly see St. Joseph's virtue. Herod is too often the unacknowl-edged elephant in the room in discussions of the Holy Family. We don't want to bring anything so unpleasant into the con-versation. Yet Herod figured in their lives in so many ways. Joseph was a carpenter; and Herod was perhaps history's most lavish patron of the craft of carpentry. Herod was pretender to the throne of David; and Joseph was a legitimate heir of that throne. Herod's daily decisions affected the wellbeing of Joseph's village, his clan, and his trade. Herod's programs and his whims exercised a profound influence on their economy and security. We can be sure that, even in remote places like Nazareth, the air was alive with whispers of news and gossip from the capital.

In the pages of the book, you'll learn about Nazareth—and how it was created almost *ex nihilo* shortly before Joseph's birth. You'll learn about religious practice and education in that place and time. You'll travel to Egypt and encounter the fascinating settlements of the Jewish people in that land. You'll also find out—in literally nuts-and-bolts terms—how a carpenter worked in those days: what tools he used, what items he crafted, where he got his training, and how he got to and from his job sites. You'll learn how large construction jobs proceeded and what role carpenters played in the work crew.

Aquilina even weaves international affairs into the story. Who knew that Cleopatra had her part to play? Who cared about the political rivalries between Syria and Egypt, Persia and Rome? Joseph knew, and he cared, because all of these matters were contributing factors in his professional life.

Then there is the religious dimension, which in Joseph's culture was bound up with everything else. This book renders first-century Jewish life in vivid terms, with carefully chosen, telling details. The author has managed to convey its complexity without bogging down the narrative with academic minutiae.

What we discover between the lines is that there were, in the first century BC, two guiding hands in history: there was the providential hand of the Lord God working God's will, and there was the demonic hand of Satan manipulating the mad King Herod. As a result, there were two rival accounts of kingship, two rival ideas of temple-building, and two rival stories of salvation. Joseph was not the only Jew to recognize this dualism, but he was perhaps the most important one. Those who recognized it were forced to make difficult choices—and face terrifying consequences.

There is so much we will never know about St. Joseph—or his wife and Divine Son—unless we come to see him in his cultural context and in contrast with the counter-narrative that centers on Herod.

In the pages of this book we see so much, so much more clearly.

Scott Hahn, PhD, is author of many books, editor of the Ignatius Catholic Study Bible, *and founder of the St. Paul Center for Biblical Theology.*

PROLOGUE
ON WORDS AND WORK

An old friend of mine—a novelist whom I much admire—asked me last week what I've been working on.

I told him, "A book about St. Joseph."

He smiled and replied: "St. Joseph is like a black hole at the center of the Gospel galaxy. You know him by his effects more than by seeing the man himself."

I know why he smiled, and I know why he compared the Guardian of the Redeemer to a black hole. St. Joseph is inaudible and all but invisible. The only record we have of his life is a few brief mentions in the New Testament. In those mentions, moreover, he says not a word.

I am not the first author to note the irony of writing a book about a man notable for his silence. Yet every year, it seems, several new titles come out. St. Joseph even has an entire *branch* of theology dedicated to the contemplation of his life. It is called Josephology, and every year Josephologists hold conferences and deliver papers—all about a man who said nothing on the record.

To sketch St. Joseph, an author must use something like the painterly technique of *chiaroscuro*. An artist depicts the surrounding shadows in order to accentuate the objects caught in a small shaft of light. The figure comes into focus because he is defined against the surrounding darkness. (It is certainly no accident that some of the masterpieces of chiaroscuro are images of St. Joseph.)

A man like St. Joseph can become indistinct when we talk too much about him. In this book, I want to talk about his world: the society and culture of the Judean kingdom, the workplaces where he practiced his craft, the villages that he called home. It was a hot climate, so we will allow him to spend his time in the shade while we contemplate his works.

I do not know if I am as skilled at my craft as St. Joseph was at his. I suspect that I am not. We can be sure, though, that he practiced his craft as well as he could. I hope that I have practiced mine as well as I can.

A note on sources: I have provided full citations for my modern sources. For ancient sources, I simply give the author of the work and its title, followed by chapter or section numbers. The ancient sources are easily accessible online in many translations. In some cases, I have modernized the English of translations made in the nineteenth century. In a few cases, I have commissioned new translations.

Throughout the book, I refer to Joseph as Jesus' father. In doing so, I follow the practice of the Blessed Virgin (Lk 2:48). I also refer to Joseph as Mary's husband, again following the pattern in Scripture (Mt 1:16, 19).

Mike Aquilina
Feast of St. Joseph
March 19, 2020

CHAPTER 1

ST. JOSEPH'S WORLD

They lived every day in alert expectation.

The people of Nazareth worked and ate and prayed; they slept and dreamed, as everyone does; but they kept a lively awareness that the Lord God was fulfilling his plan through their ordinary activities.

It was the events of recent history—the signs of the times—that had drawn their great-grandparents to move to the Holy Land from faraway Babylon. For the sake of their family's hope, the men and women of that generation had moved their households almost seven hundred miles over dusty and dangerous roads. They had founded a village in the mountains—raised it up from an overgrown wasteland.

And for the sake of that same hope, they had named their village *Nazareth*, the "Village of the Shoot," or "Village of the Twig." The pioneers from Babylon wanted everything in their new home to echo the promise the Lord God had made through the prophet Isaiah, six hundred years before: "There shall come forth a shoot from the stump of Jesse" (Is 11:1). There shall indeed come forth an anointed king—from their family.

In the century that passed between the settlement of the village and the reign of Herod, the signs seemed to come more frequently and with greater clarity. The people of Nazareth, Joseph among them, saw every indication that the time was near, or perhaps was now.

Soon the small shoot would flourish—it would rise toward heaven as a luxuriant tree and spread its branches to encompass the land and people of Israel.

It was not a question of *whether* the Lord was active in that moment of history, but rather *how* he was active—and, in particular, how he was active in their particular family, in their village, in that land.

The Lord would fulfill his promises. That had never been in doubt.

They kept careful records of their ancestry going back two thousand years, to Abraham. So they could see the pattern. It was hard to discern in the course of a year, or even a lifetime, but it was clear over the course of centuries. God made seemingly impossible promises, but he always fulfilled them.

Abraham and Sarah were in their seventies and childless, and God promised to make of them a great nation (Gn 12:2). Years passed, and angels confirmed the promise — though Sarah was now in her nineties and Abraham a hundred (Gn 17:17 and 18:10–12).

Sarah indeed bore a son, Isaac, whose offspring became a great nation.

The descendants of Abraham prospered for generations, herding and farming in the land they had been given by God. Isaac fathered Jacob, whom God renamed as Israel, and whose sons would give their names to the Twelve Tribes of Israel.

Through a series of calamitous events, the tribes found themselves transplanted to Egypt and then enslaved there. They were a people trapped by circumstance, but aware of the promise the Lord had made to their ancestors.

God called Moses, then, to deliver Israel from slavery and restore them to their ancestral land. Again, the task seemed impossible. But God assisted Moses with extraordinary events: a series of plagues visited upon the Egyptians and then a miraculous parting of the sea as the Israelites fled from Pharaoh's pursuing army.

Then, in spite of every military disadvantage, they conquered the various peoples inhabiting the land they had been promised. They took the land, cultivated it, and prospered once again.

They did so well that they wanted to have what other nations had. They wanted a king. So God gave them kings, and Israel achieved worldly greatness under their monarchy.

In the time of the first king, Saul, there appeared a young man named David, who had all the makings of a folk hero. A handsome herder of sheep, he wrote and sang songs that gained the notice of the royal household. Only David's music could calm the soul of the king. Drafted into military service, David excelled everyone on the field of battle and killed the Philistines' fiercest warrior, the gigantic Goliath. When King Saul died in battle, David was acclaimed and anointed his successor.

The nation was united under David. Like every monarch in the ancient world, he faced challenges to his rule—including an attempted coup by his son Absalom—but he overcame them in every case.

Until this time, Israel had worshipped at the tabernacle, a portable shrine that traveled from tribal land to tribal land. It held the ark of the covenant and other relics from the time of the Exodus from Egypt. David brought the shrine permanently to Jerusalem giving Israel a focal point for its worship and national identity. David himself led the procession to the capital in the vestments of a priest. He danced before the ark. He composed music for worship and earned the title "Psalmist." Most of the songs in the largest book of the Bible, the Book of Psalms, are attributed to David. His piety was as grand as all his other qualities. He ruled as a priest-king, though he was from the tribe of Judah and not the priestly tribe of Levi.

David's sins, too, were on an epic scale. He committed adultery with the wife of his most devoted guard—and then arranged for the man's murder. In order to aggrandize himself (and at the temptation of Satan, cf. 1 Chron 21:1), he ordered a census, so that he would have numbers for boasting. But his sins always drove him to abject sorrow and repentance. He established a model for penitence in his fifty-first Psalm.

Have mercy on me, O God,
according to your steadfast love;
according to your abundant mercy blot out
   my transgressions.
Wash me thoroughly from my iniquity,
and cleanse me from my sin!
For I know my transgressions,
and my sin is ever before me.
Against you, you alone, have I sinned,
and done that which is evil in your sight …
Create in me a clean heart, O God,
and put a new and right spirit within me.
Cast me not away from your presence,
and take not your holy Spirit from me.
Restore to me the joy of thy salvation,
and uphold me with a willing spirit.
—Ps 51:1–4

In David's monarchy, it seemed, the great nation descended from Abraham had arrived at its destiny. And David's son and heir, Solomon, sustained that sense of triumph. Solomon's wisdom was proverbial. He wrote books and won international renown. Monarchs came from far away to hear him speak. Fulfilling his father's wish, Solomon built a sprawling temple in Jerusalem to honor the God of Israel. Like his father, he functioned as a priest-king—not a Levite, but after the model of Melchizedek, who had ruled the city during the time of Abraham (Gn 14:18; Ps 110:4).[1]

From his father David, Solomon inherited a model of kingship, and from God he received unprecedented gifts. But he remained free to use or neglect his gifts, and he chose most unwisely. He began to adopt the style of foreign monarchs, and he even exceeded them in his conspicuous consumption. He gathered an unrivaled harem: seven hundred wives and three hundred concubines. Many of those women were foreigners, who Solomon chose in defiance of Israel's Law. They brought their strange gods to Israel and built shrines to honor them, and they enticed the king to join them in idolatrous worship. Solomon compromised and offered sacrifice at these places, egregiously violating the first of the Lord's commandments— the one on which all the other commandments depend. He chose to commit idolatry and caused grave scandal. The Lord God told him that his failings would divide the kingdom (1

---

1   On the identification of Salem with Jeru-salem, see Ps 76:1–2.

Kgs 11:11–12). Not in his lifetime, but during the reign of his successor, Israel's northern tribes rebelled and seceded, establishing their own kingdom and their own king. From Jerusalem David's heirs reigned over a much-reduced kingdom of Judah.

Then followed centuries of enmity between the two rival kingdoms—a long civil war. Family disputes are the fiercest, and all the disputants in this case were the children of Abraham. The "great nation" the patriarch had sired became a nation at war with itself.

So divided, the nation was no longer great, and the land and people were now vulnerable to incursions from neighboring armies. In the eighth century BC, the Assyrians invaded the northern lands. In the following century they pressed into Judah, but were turned back at Jerusalem. But another world power succeeded where the Assyrians had failed. The forces of Babylon took Jerusalem in 597 BC. The new conquerors rendered Judah permanently powerless by capturing its elites and deporting them to Babylon. On the way to that distant city, the last of King David's heirs, King Zedekiah, was forced to witness the execution of his sons, one by one. Then the Babylonians blinded him so that his sons' murder would be the last thing he saw (2 Kgs 25:1–7). Zedekiah spent his remaining days a prisoner in a foreign city. From all appearances, David's dynasty came to an abrupt halt at the moment of King Zedekiah's death.

What, then, to make of God's promises and the predictions of the prophets? Was it all just propaganda?

To David, God had sworn:

I will establish his line for ever
and his throne as the days of the heavens. ...
I will not violate my covenant,
or alter the word that went forth from my lips.
Once for all I have sworn by my holiness;
I will not lie to David.
His line shall endure forever,
his throne as long as the sun before me.
Like the moon it shall be established for ever;
it shall stand firm while the skies endure.
—Ps 89:29, 34–37

And this seemed only to confirm what the Patriarch Jacob had prophesied as he lay dying: "The scepter shall not depart from Judah, nor the ruler's staff from between his feet, until he comes to whom it belongs; and to him shall be the obedience of the peoples" (Gn 49:10).

The reign of David was glorious and long—forty years. Solomon ruled for another forty. That's eighty years of monarchy in a united kingdom. David's dynasty hobbled on for another four centuries. The House of David reigned for half a millennium, which is a very long time, as dynasties go, but it hardly fulfills the terms of God's promise: *as long as the sun shines and the skies endure.* And what about the "obedience of the peoples" foretold by Jacob? Quite the opposite was now true. The offspring of Judah were dispersed among the nations, subject to every ruler in the known world, but ruling over no one, not even their own people.

In Babylon, however, there lived a remnant of the family of David. We no longer have the full genealogical tables, so we do not know their line of descent.

David had fathered eighteen children with eight wives. His line presumably continued in his children other than Solomon—and then multiplied over the course of centuries. We do not know if the House of David in exile consisted of these collateral descendants.

What we do know is that the descendants of David lived as a clan while exiled in Babylon. Once kings, they now plied common trades and crafts. They kept a low profile, but within the home they passed their royal identity from one generation to the next, and they kept meticulous records of the family's genealogy.

They lived not with nostalgia, but with hope. Hope was the reason they kept the genealogies, so that the legitimate line of David could be restored at the moment of God's intervention. They were as certain of that moment as they were of any other. It was not a speculative question of *if*, but a burning question of *when*. In prayer, they echoed the prayer of their psalmist ancestor: *How long, O Lord? Will you forget us forever?* (Ps 13:1).

In Babylon they prayed, and they studied the pattern of God's salvation in the past. They marked his fulfillment, against all odds, of the promise to Abraham. They traced the course of the Exodus. And they scrutinized current events, watching for signs, examining every scrap of news that arrived from their ancestral home.

Above all, they remembered. Memory was the key to their identity, and it was the most valuable heirloom they could give to their children—the memory of the Lord's actions and interventions, the memory of the Lord's providence, the memory of the Lord's promises.

"Remember the wonderful works that he has done, his miracles, and the judgments he uttered" (Ps 105:5).

"In the sight of their fathers he wrought marvels in the land of Egypt. ... He divided the sea and let them pass through it" (Ps 78:12–13).

Remembering was the exiles' duty. Forgetting, they knew, would be their downfall as a people, their annihilation by assimilation.

Even in Babylon, God raised up prophets for the exiles who confirmed the mission of his Chosen People. Among the earliest captives to be taken there was the prophet Daniel, who foretold the nation's restoration after "seventy weeks of years" (Dn 9:24), 490 years in total. At that time an "anointed one, a prince," would arise (in Hebrew, anointed is *moshiach*, "messiah"), and that prince would reign from Jerusalem.

Jeremiah assured the people that God was already working toward that end.

> For I know the plans I have for you, says the LORD, plans for welfare and not for evil, to give you a future and a hope. Then you will call upon me and come and pray to me, and I will hear you. You will seek me and find me, ... and I will restore your fortunes and gather you from all the nations and all the places where I have driven you, says the LORD, and I will bring you back to the place from which I sent you into exile.
> —Jer 29:11–15

The opportunities for return came early. The mighty power of Babylon soon fell before the mightier power of Persia, and in 538 BC, the Persian emperor Cyrus decreed that the people of Judah (the Jews) were free to return to their land. Later in that century, another Persian emperor, Darius the Great, sponsored the rebuilding of the Jerusalem temple, which had been badly damaged at the time of the conquest.

Yet relatively few of the Jews returned to their homeland. Many were comfortable in Babylon, which was by now the only home they had known. They were making a decent living. They had never seen Jerusalem. And the resettlement of the old territory—now dilapidated and overgrown—seemed like a lot of hard work, with little promise of a return on the investment.

For the descendants of King David, perhaps the moment did not seem right. People were calling King Cyrus "the anointed one" (see Is 45:1), but he was not the princely messiah of their expectations. As long ago as Moses, it was clear that the messiah would come from the family of Abraham: "The LORD your God will raise up for you a prophet like me *from among you, from your brethren*—him you shall heed" (Dt 18:15).

So the Jews remained as exiles, strangers in a strange land, in their enclaves sorted by clan, kingly here, priestly there. They continued scrupulously to keep their records. They kept their memory alive, and with their memory, their hope.

Decades passed, and lifetimes, and centuries. Powers shifted in the region, as Alexander the Great, a Macedonian warrior, conquered the world—but Alexander died young, before he could rule what he had conquered. His generals divided the subject territories among themselves. Jerusalem went first to the Ptolemies, who were based in Egypt, and then to the Seleucids who ruled from Syria. The Seleucids were mostly benign overlords, who allowed the Jews to govern themselves and follow the Law of Moses. But the Seleucids also introduced Greek culture into Jerusalem; and there it became increasingly fashionable, especially among the urban elites, to prefer Greek customs to Jewish. The upper classes stopped following Israel's ancient dietary law and other laws.

In Babylon, the reports that arrived from Jerusalem were increasingly disturbing. During the reign of the Seleucid King Antiochus IV, the Jewish high priest was deposed and replaced by someone more congenial to Greek ways.

Then, while Antiochus was busy fighting a war in Egypt, the deposed high priest gathered a militia of a thousand men and tried to reclaim Jerusalem. Antiochus' response was swift and furious. He left Egypt with his forces and easily stormed Jerusalem. According to the Second Book of Maccabees,

> There was killing of young and old, destruction of boys, women, and children, and slaughter of virgins and infants. Within the total of three days, eighty thousand were destroyed, forty thousand in hand-to-hand fighting; and as many were sold into slavery as were slain. (2 Mc 5:13–14)

Not satisfied with wholesale slaughter, Antiochus entered the temple and plundered its treasury. On its main altar, he sacrificed a pig—the animal considered most unclean and unholy by the Jews. He had its meat boiled and then ordered his men to splash the broth on every wall in every part of the temple. It was a gross desecration, intended to shock and humiliate the Jews. It succeeded.

Antiochus believed that Judaism was a fanatical cult, incapable of compromise. Negotiation was futile, and so he imposed a policy of complete Hellenization. His goal was to eradicate every trace of Jewish identity and replace it with Greek culture. Those who resisted would be killed.

Pious families and individuals fled the city and took refuge in the remote hills. But the Seleucid forces pursued their program even into the countryside, forcing the decision on people in villages and on farms: sacrifice to idols or die.

In the wilderness of Judah, the refugees began to gain numbers and confidence. They were a ragtag group, untrained, outnumbered, and poorly armed; but they recalled the history of the Exodus and other stories of deliverance. And they began to wage a campaign of guerilla tactics. Their leader was known as Judah Maccabee—Judah the Hammer. His family, the Hasmoneans, dominated the rebel forces.

The rebellion lasted seven years, with pitched battles and raids that violated the rules of conventional warfare. The Seleucid forces were not prepared for the ferocity of their Jewish opponents. Syrian casualties ran very high. When Antiochus IV died, his army gave up and went home. His successors worked out a compromise with the Maccabees.

The Maccabees triumphantly entered Jerusalem. They purified and rededicated the temple—an event Jews still commemorate in the feast of Hanukkah. And they installed a high priest from the Hasmonean family who would also reign as king.

In faraway Babylon, in the neighborhood enclaves, the news must have incited lively discussions. What could it mean? The Jews had miraculously prevailed over their Greek overlords. They had re-established the Law of Moses as the law of the land. They were ruled by a priest-king.

In the years of Hasmonean rule, the news kept coming. The Jews recovered all the lands of the kingdom of David and Solomon, and they gave the inhabitants a choice: convert or leave. Males who stayed were forcibly circumcised.

Could this be the long-awaited time of the messiah? So many of the conditions were now in place. The span of time predicted by Daniel—the seventy weeks of years—was running down.

The Hasmoneans put out word that Jews in the dispersion should return to the traditional lands of Israel. No matter how long the families had been away, they should come home. Many from Babylon accepted the invitation and returned. This, too, was a fulfillment of prophecy: the gathering of the scattered tribes, foretold by Jeremiah.

Large groups within the clan of King David made the decision to move. They packed their households into wagons and onto beasts. They carefully stowed the books of the genealogies. Then they launched their caravan upon a journey of almost seven hundred miles.

According to today's method of calculating dates, the year was approximately 100 BC.

The returnees from the House of David acquired two large tracts in lower Galilee—land that had been uninhabited for almost six hundred years.[2] They established two villages there and gave both of them names strongly associated with the anticipated messiah.

One they named *Kochba*, the Village of the Star, evoking the oracle of the prophet Balaam: "I see him, but not now; I behold him, but not nigh: a star shall come forth out of Jacob" (Nm 24:17).

The other site they named *Nazareth*, the Village of the Shoot, as we saw at the beginning of this chapter. "There shall come forth a shoot from the stump of Jesse."

The family of David was intensely aware of their mission and purpose in history. The residents of Nazareth and Kochba were alive to the possibility—perhaps a probability—that one of them would bear the messiah into the world.

Archeologists estimate that Nazareth had 120–150 inhabitants in the mid-first century before Christ.[3] Seventy years

2   Bargil Pixner, "Jesus and His Community: Between Essenes and Pharisees," in J. H. Charlesworth and Loren L. Johns, eds., *Hillel and Jesus: Comparative Studies of Two Major Religious Leaders*, (Minneapolis, MN: Fortress, 1997), 214.

3   Pixner, 214.

after the clan's arrival, they were surely established in their routines and integrated into the local economy. The households had their trades, which fathers taught their sons, and mothers taught their daughters.

Later in that century, one of the families in Nazareth—a family of artisans—gave birth to a boy and named him Joseph. His name, like the name of his birthplace, reflected the hope of his people. Joseph, in Hebrew, means "God will increase."

CHAPTER 2

JOSEPH AND HIS KING

The Hasmoneans rode into Jerusalem on a wave of rage. Antiochus IV had profaned what was most sacred to religiously observant Jews, and in doing so, he provoked an earthquake of indignation. Even people who had been waxing indifferent were offended by his violent blasphemy.

To the desecration of the temple he added the massacre of tens of thousands—and then he extended his persecution from the city into the countryside. His soldiers ruthlessly executed the sentence until it seemed that every family was seething to avenge its lost members.

The Hasmoneans' militia, the Maccabees, battled for high ideals such as piety and patriotism; and it is easier to fight—and recruit—for a cause that is clearly righteous.

The Hasmoneans were not, however, prepared for victory. More precisely, they were not ready for what follows after victory. Nothing in their experience had prepared them for ruling.

They were spontaneous rebels who had managed to unseat a tyrant. Now, as winners, they continued to do what they had already done well—but they turned that skill against one another. They involved themselves in family conflict, palace intrigue, and plots and schemes to displace one another. Once warriors for God, they soon seemed bored with matters of prayer and sacred worship. Though they exercised priesthood as their office demanded, they were capable of shockingly casual impiety.

Consider Alexander Jannaeus. He was most likely the reigning king and high priest when the descendants of King David arrived from Babylon. He ruled for more than a quarter-century, in which time he strengthened the military and expanded the territory under Jerusalem's control. But he faced intermittent resistance from his subjects, which sometimes exploded into full rebellion.

Though he was high priest, he was not above manipulating religious sentiment and exploiting divisions. In Judea at the time, there were three dominant factions to pit against each other.[4]

4   For more about these groups, see James C. VanderKam, *An Introduction to Early Judaism* (Grand Rapids, MI: Eerdmans, 2001), 186–192; Jacob Neusner, *Judaism in the Beginning of Christianity* (Philadelphia: Fortress Press, 1984), 25–28; Günter Stemberger, *Jewish Contemporaries of Jesus: Pharisees, Sadducees, Essenes* (Minneapolis, MN: Fortress, 1995); and Stephen M. Wylen, *The Jews in the Time of Jesus: An Introduction* (Mahwah, NJ: Paulist, 1996), 133–147.

The Sadducees, the descendants of Zadok, were the clerical caste, from whom the high priest had formerly been chosen. They were wealthy and largely materialist in their approach to religion. They disbelieved in angels and the afterlife. They recognized only the five books of Moses, the Torah, as Scripture.

The Pharisees were a lay movement that emphasized the meticulous observance of the Law. They supplemented the statutes of Moses with other regulations based on customs and oral tradition. They recognized as authoritative, in addition to the Torah, the Prophets, the Psalms, and sacred writings of Israel.

The Essenes were a group of pious separatists, founded probably when the Seleucids deposed the legitimate high priest and replaced him with his brother. They considered themselves the keepers of the traditional, priestly, sacrificial faith, and they awaited a messiah (or perhaps two messiahs) who would restore the integrity of Israel's religious institutions. The Essenes had a contemplative community in the Judean desert.

Alexander Jannaeus favored the Sadducees, though his wife was from a family of Pharisees. The Sadducees supported King Alexander consistently—and confirmed his legitimacy as high priest when the Pharisees called it into question. The Pharisees, confident in their popularity with the common folk, showed Alexander increasing contempt; and he returned the favor.

All the males in Israel were required to make pilgrimage to Jerusalem for three festivals every year: Passover, Pentecost, and Sukkoth (the Feast of Booths). In 93 BC, Alexander appeared at the temple to perform his high-priestly duties. To show his disdain for the Pharisees, he intentionally defied the norms they had prescribed for the ritual. Instead of pouring water onto the altar, he poured it on his own feet.

This shocked and enraged the enormous crowd that swelled the city. They expected such disrespect from Greek overlords, but not from their high priest and king. They raised their voices in mockery against Alexander, who then ordered the military to take action.

A massacre ensued, and six thousand were dead by the end of the festival. The episode triggered a civil war, which Alexander suppressed brutally. When he was sure he had succeeded, he brought the captive rebels back *en masse* to Jerusalem, and he sentenced eight hundred of them, mostly Pharisees, to crucifixion. While they hung dying on their crosses, Alexander had their wives and children brought out. Then the crucified men watched as soldiers slit the throats of their loved ones.

Alexander, meanwhile, sat nearby, eating and drinking with his concubines.

The Hasmoneans were appalling tyrants, capable of commanding respect only by force. They had won the land through the strength of the pious—but then they regularly found occasions to alienate the pious.

Keenly aware of their unpopularity, they ruled uneasily, obsessive and suspicious, searching out and trying to quash the next attempted coup or rebellion.

It must have been a worrisome time for the descendants of King David. Even in their remote villages, their existence could be a provocation. Who could question their legitimacy? They were bred for kingship and royal priesthood. They believed themselves to be the vessels of the messiah. And none of this was secret. It was advertised in the very names of their villages.

The restored lands of Israel sat precariously between two rival powers, Egypt and Syria, both ruled by the constantly quarreling descendants of the generals of Alexander the Great. But the world map was shifting, and new powers were eclipsing the old. Rome was extending imperial control to the west of the Holy Land, and Persia was encroaching from the East.

The lands ruled by Jerusalem were in a key position. Their sea plain provided the only thoroughfare for commercial or military activity, and the Hasmoneans used this position to their advantage.

As far back as the days of Judah Maccabee, the Hasmoneans pursued close diplomatic ties with Rome. In fact, the First Book of Maccabees names the kingdom's bond with the Romans not as an alliance, but as "friendship" (1 Mc 12:1).

Such friendship won significant military and economic support. With Rome's help, the Judean kingdom grew increasingly independent of outside interference.[5] And this continued for several decades, until Rome tired of the game.

The depravity of the Hasmoneans only inflamed the popular expectation of a messiah. Though they were execrable sinners, they were clearly amassing power for God's people. Their dynasty was comparable, perhaps, to the reign of King Saul, which preceded the reign of King David. Saul was insane, jealous, and despotic; he brashly disobeyed the direct commands of God; he brought about his own catastrophic downfall. And yet, in hindsight, it was clear that he had prepared the way for the Golden Age under King David.

The seventy weeks of years had almost run down. The Hasmoneans were loathsome indeed, but they could not thwart the plan of God.

Yet the Almighty's ways are mysterious. In 67 BC, the Hasmoneans were having their usual dispute over succession. Two brothers, Hyrcanus and Aristobulus, went to war over the

5   Chris Seeman, *Rome and Judea in Transition: Hasmonean Relations with the Roman Republic and the Evolution of the High Priesthood* (New York: Peter Lang, 2013), 272, 367.

throne, and their rivalry threatened to destabilize the entire region. Rome feared the encroachment of Persia and the loss of free passage through Judea.

In 63 BC, the Roman general Pompey settled the dispute. With a massive force, he laid siege to Jerusalem. When the inevitable victory came, he imposed tribute on Judea. He demoted the monarchy. And he restored order countrywide by severe measures. Afterward, the Hasmoneans could no longer pretend to be independent.

They continued, however, to bicker and plot against one another. In 37 BC, the Romans tired of the arrangement, and in July of that year the forces of a local Edomite warlord, backed by Rome, laid siege to Jerusalem and then took the city. The Hasmonean King Antigonus was captured, and the Romans ordered him decapitated.

If the Pharisees had fussed about the pedigree of the Hasmoneans, how should they feel now—ruled by an Edomite, a Gentile by birth, imposed by Gentiles from faraway Rome? The young king—he was in his mid-thirties—assured his subjects that he was one of them. He had undergone circumcision, and he observed the Law of Moses.

The people searched for God's will even in those strange new developments. They could not deny the prodigies of the new king, this Edomite named Herod.

For Herod was a canny and valiant military leader. He was physically strong, with undeniable charisma. He was unsurpassed as a diplomat, a friend to the great figures on the world stage. He dared to do business with Julius Caesar, Cassius, Marc Antony, Cleopatra, and Caesar Augustus—and he usually got what he wanted! To his Jewish subjects, he presented himself as a Jew. To his Roman patrons, he was always a "Friend of Rome."

In due time he took for himself a wife from the Hasmonean line, a move intended to make him still more acceptable to his subjects. But they remained wary. It bothered him, but he couldn't let their diffidence distract him. He had work to do.

Herod was often on the move. He placed a premium on law and order. He suppressed banditry along the roads, and so removed one of the great constraints on commerce and travel. His easy relations with Rome ensured that his kingdom received regular benefices from the capital. Imports flowed in; exports flowed out.

He ruled with skill, efficiency, confidence, and competence—qualities that none of the Hasmoneans had been able to muster all at once. But there was another side to Herod. When he was young, he was prone to long spells of suicidal depression.[6] As he grew older and gained power, his depression turned to murderous rage, directed almost randomly at friends and foes. His handlers were careful to hide these

---

6   William J. Gross, *Herod the Great* (Baltimore: Helicon, 1962), 111.

periods of debility from the people. When the king vanished from sight, he was said to be away on a hunting expedition.

Herod worked to earn the respect and affection of his people, and still they scorned him. He was keenly aware of their expectations. Speculation about the messiah was the common conversation throughout the land. Perhaps, Herod thought, he could stake a credible claim to the title.

He minted coins that presented his name along with a star[7], one of the two common symbols of the messiah, the other being the shoot of Jesse. According to one account, he put the question to the teachers of the Law in Jerusalem: Could he be the long-awaited one?

The scholars noted the recent fulfillment of many prophecies. Jacob had predicted the constancy of Judah's rule—and now the monarchy was returned to the land of Judah. Daniel had forecast a king who would reign in seventy weeks of years—and here, in Herod, was a king arriving almost exactly at that moment. Certain indications were there. And yet, according to the histories, the scholars could not bring themselves to endorse Herod as the messiah.

The greatest obstacle was one he could never overcome: He was foreign-born. The Torah was clear on this matter:

7   Étienne Nodet, 'The Slavonic Version of the *Jewish War* of Josephus" in Tom Holmén and Stanley E. Porter, eds., *Handbook for the Study of the Historical Jesus* (Leiden: Brill, 2011), 1531–1532.

You may indeed set a king over you him whom the
LORD your God will choose. *One from among your
brethren you shall set as king* over you; *you may not
put a foreigner over you*, who is not your brother. (Dt
17:15, emphasis added)

When word of this rejection reached Herod, his response
was swift and simple. He had the councilors massacred. He
spared the life of one man, Baba ben Buta, because of his value
as a royal advisor—though, for good measure, he had the man
blinded, so that in the future he would learn to temper his
advice to Herod's wishes.[8]

Nevertheless, Herod succeeded in persuading some in his
kingdom. The desire for the messiah was so strong that even
a homicidal candidate seemed better than no candidate at all.
Besides, hadn't King David arranged the killing of Uriah the
Hittite, his rival for Bathsheba's affection? If David was legitimate in spite of one murder, couldn't the true messiah be
granted a few of his own?

There arose a faction known as the Herodians, who
accepted Herod's messianic claims. They were something more
than a political party, but less than a religious sect. They per-
severed even after the king's death, when they extended the
messianic title to his successors. The Herodians appear occa-
sionally in the New Testament (see Mk 3:6, 12:13; Mt 22:16).

---

8   Gross, 127.

According to St. Jerome and St. Epiphanius, they endured among the Jews at least into the late fourth century AD, still awaiting their vindication.[9]

We have no record of how the House of David received the news of these events. Given their firm belief in the royal destiny of their own family, it is difficult to imagine their throwing support behind King Herod. Yet, there is no evidence that they considered rebellion or plotted an overthrow. Herod's suspicions blossomed into paranoia over time, and he had a vast network of spies cast everywhere in the kingdom. The spies were rewarded for their discoveries, so they tended to find plots even where there were none. Herod acted on many such whispers, visiting death on many families. Yet there is no record of a pogrom against the descendants of David. They apparently presented no credible threat, even though they possessed the most persuasive claim to the throne.[10]

They may have appeared too small and weak. Or maybe they just never drew attention to themselves. They devoted themselves not to futile rebellion, but to the quiet care of their

---

9   See St. Jerome, *Dialogue Against the Luciferians*, 23 and Epiphanius, *Panarion*, 1.20.1–2. See also Pseudo-Tertullian, *Against All Heresies*, 1.1.

10   For the Davidic identity of the messiah, see Peter Schäfer, *The Jewish Jesus: How Judaism and Christianity Shaped Each Other* (Princeton, NJ: Princeton University Press, 2012), 223–226.

families, leaving the rest to God. Their recent ancestors had lived for centuries under the rule of Babylonians and Persians, who made no pretense of Judaism. How were they worse off under Herod?

They could not, however, have entirely avoided the conversation about the messiah. Speculation was universal and urgent. His imminent arrival was a point on which Pharisees, Sadducees, and Essenes seemed to agree—though with important shades of difference.

In the villages inhabited by David's clan, pregnant mothers were surely reminded, quietly, that *this* child could be the one. Small children were raised with the virtues and skills modeled by their ancestors, the kings. They had to be brave for battle, like David. They should be wise and discerning, like Solomon. They should be zealous for true worship, like Hezekiah. It would not be surprising if descendants of the Psalmist received musical training as well.

Joseph of Nazareth was born in these times and born *for* these times. Surely the question arose from someone at his birth: *Could he be the one?*

Scholars and saints disagree about Joseph's birthdate. Some say he was born long before Herod took the throne; others say he was born more than a decade afterward. In any case, we know that Joseph died sometime between 8 AD and 30 AD , and he lived a significant portion of his life under Herod's rule. Perhaps it was most of his life, or the prime of his life, or his most formative years. In any event, we know that the paths of Herod and Joseph were destined to converge.

CHAPTER 3

PROSPERITY AND ITS PRICE

Though he suffered the contempt of his subjects, Herod was—even in his own lifetime—known as "Herod the Great." His greatness at first was manifest in a robust economy. He was not idly boasting when he said, "With God's assistance, I have advanced the nation of the Jews to a degree of happiness which they never had before."[11] Not even under David and Solomon had the people prospered so magnificently. Through his deliberate efforts, Herod transformed the landscape. No longer did Judea look like a second-rate power. No longer did Jerusalem look like a backwater town. The people could be justly proud of their land and its recent accomplishments.

---

11   Josephus, *Antiquities of the Jews* 15.11.

Herod saw the way foreign leaders earned prestige and praise. They made an overpowering impression through building monuments: They raised mighty towers, obelisks, and arches. They drained swamps, and on the reclaimed land they built stadiums, theaters, and racetracks for the entertainment of their people.

From his youth, Herod showed himself to be a prodigy in two distinct areas: architectural design and institutional terror. Too often in discussions of the despot, scholars slight the former because of a fascination with the latter. But they were part of the same program of self-aggrandizement and nation building. His goal was always the same: to command awe, respect, fear.

He built cities where mere villages had stood before. He raised enormous public works, including aqueducts, fortresses, reservoirs, and a manmade harbor at the seaport. He built grand complexes for entertainment and shopping. One of his modern biographers noted, "Herod, however rapidly his cities sprang up, always built, as he hoped, for posterity. Imperishable stone was his medium, possible expansion was provided for, nothing was skimped or cheapened."[12] He consulted with the Roman Vitruvius, who established the principles of classical architecture and wrote the first textbook. And Herod funded projects abroad as well as at home. His boulevard in Antioch was the first of its kind—paved with polished marble

---

12   Gross, 228.

and lined with streetlamps and market stalls. It was imitated in major cities for centuries afterward. Still today, Herod is credited with several world records, including largest palace ever built, largest plaza, and largest royal portico.[13]

His masterpiece, however, was the Jerusalem temple. For this, he spared no expense. It was his great chance to declare his piety toward the God of Israel—and prove that his conversion was authentic, that he was truly one with his people. He recruited more than a thousand builders from priestly families. His supervisors made sure that only consecrated hands would tear down or build up any part of the sacred edifice. In less than two years of construction, the greater part of the project was completed, though the detail work continued for another eighty years. The result was magnificent, unrivaled in the world. The people of Judea were stunned and pleased.

Yet, they still despised Herod. He cut their taxes by a third, and they showed him contempt.

It's hard to know, at this remove, whether it was the people's loathing for him that fueled his insecurity, or his suspicion that made them loathe him. It seems to have been a closed system, sure to perpetuate itself for as long as he was alive.

A master diplomat, he would present a friendly face until the moment he didn't; and by then it was too late, because then the violence began. He arranged the murder of three of

13   Magen Broshi, "King on a Shrink's Couch," *Haaretz*, June 29, 2007. Retrieved from Haaretz.com March 1, 2020.

his sons, one brother-in-law, his mother-in-law, and the most beloved of his ten wives.

Nevertheless, while flouting the commandment against killing, Herod strove to keep up the appearance of Jewish observance. He scrupulously avoided pork and other non-kosher foods. The situation inspired his patron, Caesar Augustus, to remark, "It's safer to be Herod's sow than Herod's son."[14] In his later years, said one biographer, "he would … never be far from the border of insanity."[15]

Most of what we know about Herod, we know from the first-century Jewish historian Josephus, who had access to a wealth of documentary records. We can fill out his account with the impressions of a handful of Roman historians, who chronicled Herod's visits to their city and his interactions with Marc Antony and Augustus.

We know Herod also from a few details in the opening chapters of St. Matthew's Gospel. This early Christian source conforms rather exactly to all we see in the pages of the historians. In Matthew as in Josephus, Herod appears as paranoid, obsessed, insecure, jealous, and violent.

Herod spent his reign in the limelight.

---

14   Macrobius, *Saturnalia* 2.4.11.

15   Gross, 206.

Joseph, meanwhile, grew up in obscurity. Even his parentage is unclear. The New Testament gives two genealogies of Jesus, and they seem to be in conflict about the identity of Joseph's father. St. Matthew states that Joseph's father was named Jacob (Mt 1:16), while St. Luke lists him as Heli (Lk 3:23). Neither genealogy provides a complete list of generations without gaps, so it's possible that one (or both) has simply skipped the generation immediately before Joseph.

But we have another account from an historian named Sextus Julius Africanus. He lived in the Holy Land in the second century and had contact with the family of Jesus and the villages of David's descendants. Africanus reports that Joseph's mother was left a childless widow when her husband Heli died. By Jewish law (Dt 25:5–10), Heli's brother Jacob was required to marry her and "raise up children for his brother," Heli. (See Mk 12:19 for a demonstration of the process.) In such arrangements, known as levirate marriages, both men would be known as the child's father.[16]

The other matter that generates passionate disagreement is the date of Joseph's birth. This problem arises not from the Gospels, but rather from later devotional literature and Christian works of fiction. The New Testament presents the adult Joseph as a man of strength and vigor. He makes a journey

---

16   Africanus' material is preserved in Eusebius, *Church History*, 1.7.2–16; see also the discussion in Oskar Skarsaune and Reidar Hvalvik, *Jewish Believers in Jesus: The Early Centuries* (Peabody, MA: Hendrickson, 2007), 352–353.

of nearly a thousand miles, from Judea to Egypt, presumably on foot or by donkey, fleeing from squads of Herod's soldiers. Three decades later, Joseph—by then deceased—is still remembered for practicing a trade that demanded physical strength and agility (See Mt 13:55 and Mk 6:3.). The New Testament, then, presents a clear, consistent witness that Joseph married as a young man.

Later apocryphal works, however, were primarily concerned with defending Mary's virginal conception. They wanted to leave no room for doubt, and so they portrayed Joseph as a very old man, infirm and decrepit. The earliest document to do this was the immensely popular *Gospel of Mary*, written in the early second century and later titled the *Protoevangelium of James*. Other apocrypha followed, each outdoing the last in the silliness of its claims. The Coptic *History of Joseph the Carpenter* presents Joseph as ninety-one-years old at his wedding to Mary—with grandchildren who are older than his bride![17]

These accounts are most charitably dismissed as well-intentioned fictions. Conjured up for apologetic purposes, they have no basis in fact. (St. Jerome and St. Thomas Aquinas denounced them in much stronger terms.) We know precious little about Joseph from reliable historical sources, but

---

17   See Joseph T. Lienhard, SJ, *St. Joseph in Early Christianity: A Study and an Anthology of Patristic Texts* (Philadelphia, PA: St. Joseph's University Press, 1999), 9–10.

what we do know seems to rule out the claim that he was an elderly man.

Thus, we proceed from the assumption that he was born and grew up during the reign of Herod. The Gospels use the Greek word *tekton* to describe him, a term that was most commonly applied to manual laborers who worked with wood, stone, or metal. Reliable ancient traditions tell us that Joseph and his son, Jesus, were carpenters.[18]

As Jesus learned his trade from Joseph, so Joseph probably had learned it from his father. This was the ordinary way of vocational and professional training. A household of craftsmen was a business enterprise. The Talmud preserves the ancient counsel: "A man has a duty to teach his son a trade. ... Anyone who does not teach his son a trade, teaches him to steal."[19]

Joseph would have grown up watching the members of his extended family as they worked. In their tiny village, perhaps the craftsmen had a common work area, enclosed by walls or covered with a canopy. It seems likely that those who were builders by trade would construct a workspace that sheltered them from the elements and made work possible in all weather.

There were no power tools, of course, so carpentry required strong arms, a keen eye, and skill with a variety of

---

18   See, for example, St. Justin Martyr, *Dialogue with Trypho*, 88.

19   Talmud, *Kiddushin*, 29a.

implements: "axes, chisels, drills, saws, squares, hammers, and plumb lines."[20]

For the people in his village, Joseph and his kin probably produced furniture and basic tools for farming and housekeeping. A small workshop might also make waterwheels for irrigation and fences for the containment of livestock.

Typically, however, such piecework took up only a small portion of a carpenter's time. In a large shop, it may have been delegated routinely to young family members. The grown men were much in demand during the reign of Herod the Great. There were cities within walking distance—Sepphoris was only four miles away—and the cities had many large construction projects. Crews would typically set out before dawn and make the return trip at dusk. Once home, they ate and slept; and the next day, they set out on foot, again. If the projects were urgent—or farther than a few miles away—they would camp at the worksite.

The demand for artisans was universal during Joseph's childhood and youth. Carpenters from Judea even had opportunities to travel abroad for construction. But there was more than enough work close to home. Herod himself valued the skills of men who worked in construction. They were essential to his propaganda—his legacy and his international stature.

---

20   D.A. Fiensy, "Jesus' Socioeconomic Background," in J. H. Charlesworth and Loren L. Johns, eds., *Hillel and Jesus: Comparative Studies of Two Major Religious Leaders* (Minneapolis, MN: Fortress, 1997), 247.

And he was known to pay very well. There is evidence that a craftsman could even grow rich in those times. One of Joseph's contemporaries was a man named "Simon the Temple Builder," whose opulent tomb and ossuary have only recently been discovered.

For every one of Herod's construction projects, carpenters had to be busy at their task before the others arrived on the scene — long before the stonemasons and earthmovers. It was the carpenters who built the wagons, scaffolding, cranes, and ladders that made possible the work of the other men. And when the time arrived for the other men to get busy, the carpenters *stayed* busy, now installing vaults and beams and walkways.

Craftsmen in Herod's kingdom could usually speak two languages with some degree of fluency: their native Aramaic, as well as Greek, which was the common language of business and government in the Mediterranean region. In their work-related travels, they were exposed to urban culture. They had regular interactions with clients who were quite wealthy and who valued their craft.

They were not poor—at least not by the standard of their time. According to biblical scholar David Fiensy,

> These workers were able, because of their skills, to demand a higher wage than the ordinary unskilled day laborer, yet they were usually not as comfortable as the merchants … [M]ost artisans worked hard,

but were able to earn just enough to live simply.
They were not usually wealthy but neither were
they starving.[21]

Let us imagine that Joseph and his father were especially
skilled at their craft. It seems likely, since Joseph was known
even after death as "*the* carpenter." If so, they must have had
many opportunities for work. They had to weigh offers, negoti-
ate terms, schedule trips, and collect payments. Even in conditions that are primitive by today's standards, these basic tasks
had to get done, or the family went hungry.

A good reputation would be essential to the family business. Excellence brought attention, and attention
brought clients.

Excellence, though, could also draw envy from those who
were less excellent. Herod's regime relied upon builders and
craftsmen, but also upon spies and informants. If Herod valued his builders, you can bet his spies were often lurking
about and looking into the lives of individual artisans. To be
noticed for one's work is always a wonderful thing; but during
a reign of terror it can also be a very dangerous thing.

It was dangerous enough to be known as a descendant of
King David. As such, both Joseph and his father were vulnerable. A snitch could cast them as rivals to Herod, even though

---

they were manual laborers. David, after all, was a shepherd boy when the prophet Samuel singled him out for anointing.

These were challenging times to do business.

Joseph's world was unlike ours in most ways, but most strikingly perhaps in its unity of life. Religion was not compartmentalized. Religious activity was not relegated to a particular place or a certain day of the week, but rather, it was pervasive, touching upon every aspect of life at home and on the job.

There certainly would have been a synagogue in Nazareth, and a service would have been conducted there on the Sabbath. The liturgy involved prayers, readings from the Law and Prophets, and then interpretation of the Scriptures by a teacher.

Significant rites of passage took place at the synagogue. On the eighth day after birth, male babies were circumcised there. When a boy was able to read, he was permitted to read for the first time from the Torah; as he read, a spoonful of honey was placed in his mouth, so that the memory of reading the Law would always be sweet. At twelve or thirteen, a boy was expected to assume the full obligations of the Law of Moses: fasting, prayer, pilgrimage, and the activity of the synagogue.

The synagogue also served as a civic gathering place and a hostel for Jewish travelers. Governing the local synagogue were elders, priests, and usually a single leader, an *archisynagogos*, who managed day-to-day activity there. In the modern world, synagogues can vary much, depending on their denominational affiliations—Orthodox, Conservative, Reform, or Reconstructionist. In the ancient world as well, synagogues could differ from one village to the next, depending on the religious movement that dominated the local scene—the Pharisees, Sadducees, or Essenes.

There was no sacrificial liturgy at the synagogue. The temple in Jerusalem was the only place on earth where valid sacrifice could be offered to the God of Israel. Adult males were required to make pilgrimage there three times a year on the major feasts.

But ritual prayers were offered at home as well. And the regulations of the Torah governed a family's diet, work, and leisure, and a married couple's sexual relations.

The reign of Herod the Great—strangely enough—coincided with a period of religious ferment in the land. Judaism's two great teachers, Hillel and Shammai, were alive and active in Jerusalem. With their scholarship and piety, they set standards for Jewish thought for all generations afterward. With the reconstruction of the temple came a great renewal of liturgical life—and an intensification of the experience of pilgrimage.

The Pharisees had shown fortitude during the reign of the Hasmoneans. They were fearless in opposing religious abuses of the monarchs. They continued, intermittently, to be an irritant to Herod.

The Essenes—strangely enough—found favor with Herod. His childhood tutor was a member of the monastic movement, and Herod retained him as a close advisor during his reign. Yet the Essenes remained outliers. They rejected as illicit all the high priests since the early Hasmoneans, and they refused to recognize any ritual changes enacted by those priests. So they kept their own calendars and observed the feasts in their own ways. They made pilgrimage to Jerusalem, but did not partake in the temple sacrifices. Some Essenes lived in Jerusalem. A large number lived in community in the desert by the Dead Sea. The community followed a strict ascetical regime, and it included both celibate and married members.

An increasing number of scholars believe that the family of Jesus had contact with the Essenes. St. John the Baptist spent time in the desert and shared the movement's emphases on asceticism and the coming age of the messiah. Mary and Joseph, too, approached their marriage in ways that seem to conform to Essene asceticism. Mary's responses to the angel during the Annunciation make sense only if she had intended to observe lifelong virginity. Reviewing the evidence, the archeologist Bargil Pixner concluded that Joseph's family "had strong ties with the Essene movement."[22] John Bergsma, in his book *Jesus and the Dead Sea Scrolls*, arrived at a similar conclusion.[23]

It is quite possible that Joseph grew up with a keen awareness of the imminence of the messiah's arrival—and the likelihood that the messiah would come from Joseph's own family. He also grew up with vocational options he had to sort out and discern for himself.

In early adolescence, Joseph would have been expected to live an adult faith. Presumably, he would also be bearing an adult's share in the labor that supported the household. Even young men were expected to work hard six days every week. Rest came on the seventh day, the Sabbath, and was strictly enforced. That day was reserved entirely for prayer and contemplative leisure; nothing resembling labor was permitted.

Marriages were arranged by parents, with counsel from other adults and the consent of the couple to be joined. A modern Jewish scholar, Samuel Sandmel, emphasized the difference between ancient and modern ideas of marriage. Among the Jews in the first century, "marriage was viewed as a solemn business arrangement between groom and bride and their families."[24] The ancient rabbis recommended that men should marry by age eighteen. Girls were encouraged to marry

22   Pixner, 213.

23   John Bergsma, *Jesus and the Dead Sea Scrolls* (New York: Image, 2019), 22–27.

24   Samuel Sandmel, *Judaism and Christian Beginnings* (New York: Oxford, 1978), 193.

shortly after menarche, the first occurrence of menstruation, ordinarily in their early teens.

One's mate was usually chosen from within the clan or village. This ensured a basic similarity of customs, diet, values, and religious understanding. In a village as tiny as Nazareth, all the young people would have known each other very well by the time they were old enough to marry. The *total* population of Nazareth was far smaller than the average high school graduating class in twenty-first-century America.

Sometimes parents made marriage arrangements when the children involved were quite young. Years later, when the couple came of age, their union would be solemnized with *erusin*, a betrothal or engagement. The families involved would write up formal terms and specify the gifts and possessions involved in the transaction. After betrothal, the bond could be broken only by divorce. The marriage was final, and normally consummated, only after a ceremony called *kiddushin* (sanctities).

It is possible that Joseph and Mary knew from a very early age that they were intended for one another. It is possible, too, that a young couple, influenced by Essene asceticism, could commit themselves to continence within marriage.

CHAPTER 4
MARRIAGE AMID THE MADNESS

As Herod passed the age of sixty, his ailments, both physical and mental, grew more severe. His contemporaries recorded his symptoms in horrifying detail, and medical historians today use these records to diagnose him from across the millennia. Some speculate that he suffered from arteriosclerosis, the thickening and hardening of the walls of his arteries. It was common then, as it is now; but it was untreatable then. In his later sixties he seems to have suffered from chronic kidney disease, which made him itch constantly all over his body. This was further complicated, perhaps, by a sexually transmitted disease that left him with maggot-infested gangrene. In his last two years, he may have suffered all these maladies at the same time.

Mentally, he had never been well. From his youth, he was tempted to suicide. He would sometimes fall into catatonic states. He suffered severe paranoia, which was fed constantly by schemers and spies. His paranoia drove him to binges of murderous violence. From all accounts, it seems that his murder of Mariamne, his beloved second wife, plunged him into a guilty depression from which he never fully recovered. Herod's final years were a rage of pain for Herod—and a dangerous ordeal for anyone who lived close to him.

As Joseph and Mary prepared to wed, they were surely pleased to live in obscurity in Nazareth, almost 150 miles from Herod's capital—and even further from his private fortress, where he would retire when his madness was in bloom.

They had hardly made their betrothal, however, when strange things began to happen. Young Mary received a visit from an angel. An ancient tradition holds that this took place as she drew water from the village well.[25] The angel made it clear to Mary that she would soon be pregnant by the power of God, that her baby would be known as the Son of God, and that he would indeed be the Messiah: "The Lord God will give to him the throne of his father David, and he will reign over the house of Jacob for ever; and of his kingdom there will be no end" (Lk 1:32–33).

---

25   See Michael Peppard, "Is This the Oldest Image of the Virgin Mary?" *New York Times*, January 30, 2016. Retrieved from NYTimes.com March 1, 2020.

The angel's words were measured precisely to match the expectations held by someone born to the House of David. And the ancient witnesses are unanimous in their testimony that Mary, like Joseph, was a descendant of the king.[26]

Mary's ancestry, though, was priestly as well as royal. The Gospel of Luke implies as much in the verses that follow the angel's announcement, as Mary prepares to visit her pregnant kinswoman Elizabeth. Elizabeth is married to a priest named Zechariah, who serves at the altar in the Jerusalem temple. Mary's journey, then, will take her to Ein Karem, a village in the hills outside the capital.

The journey would have taken several days by foot, slightly less in a cart or on the back of a beast. Travelers could find a place to rest at synagogues along the way, and even sleep there overnight. Mary had made the journey before, and the itinerary was surely familiar to her. Since she was betrothed to Joseph, it seems likely that he would have accompanied her this time, for safety's sake, and then returned to Nazareth after he had delivered her to Zechariah and Elizabeth.

Joseph was her kinsman. He had been her trusted friend for years. He was her fiancé, already legally bound to her for life. She could hardly have withheld her news from him.

---

26   See St. Ignatius of Antioch, *Letter to the Ephesians*, 18.2; St. Justin Martyr, *Dialogue with Trypho*, 45.4; and *Protoevangelium of James*, 10.1.

Joseph's response to Mary has been the source of much dispute since the earliest days of Christianity. In English translation of the New Testament, it appears as a single sentence spread over two verses.

> Now the birth of Jesus Christ took place in this way. When his mother Mary had been betrothed to Joseph, before they came together she was found to be with child of the Holy Spirit; and her husband Joseph, being a just man and unwilling to put her to shame, resolved to send her away quietly.
> —Mt 1:18–19

The narrative gives a cold accounting of the facts and the acts of will. Any reader, however, would assume that Joseph must have endured torrents of emotion as he faced his decision. There is merely the hint of an interior drama that must have seemed unbearable to Joseph. But what exactly were his emotions? What was the drama? What was the choice he considered that led him to resolve to divorce Mary?

Commentators down the ages have proposed three approaches to this enigmatic passage: (1) the suspicion theory, (2) the perplexity theory, and (3) the reverence theory.[27] Let us examine them briefly.

---

27   See the commentary on this Gospel passage in Scott Hahn and Curtis Mitch, *Ignatius Catholic Study Bible* (San Francisco, CA: Ignatius Press, 2010).

1. The Suspicion Theory. In this reading of the Gospel passage, Joseph suspects that Mary has been unfaithful. He is devastated, but his love for her remains so great that he cannot bear the thought of her facing public shame—or, worse, the death penalty, since adultery was a capital crime, punishable by stoning. He decides to divorce her, as the Law permitted, until an angel deters him from that course of action.

2. The Perplexity Theory. According to this theory, Joseph cannot understand what has happened. He does not believe Mary could be unfaithful. Yet her pregnancy is undeniable and subject to legal penalties. Since Joseph is a just man, he finds a solution that respects the Law, but protects Mary as well. The angel, in this reading, provides the information that Joseph lacks and helps him to make a plan for going forward.

3. The Reverence Theory. This third theory presents Joseph as a man overwhelmed by awe when he learns of Mary's miraculous conception. From the beginning, he knows of God's singular intervention: "she was found *to be with child of the Holy Spirit.*" Joseph feels unworthy to be involved, and so he decides he will cooperate just long enough to protect Mary's secret and then make a quiet exit. In this reading, Joseph's first impulse is like St. Peter's when he said to Jesus, "Depart from me!" (Lk 5:8), or the Centurion's when he said, "I am not worthy to have you come under my roof" (Lk 7:6). The angel, however, persuades Joseph to put aside his fears.

Each theory has saints and doctors of the church among its proponents. St. Justin Martyr and St. Augustine of Hippo advanced the first; St. Jerome the second; and St. Thomas Aquinas, St. Bernard of Clairvaux, and St. Josemaria Escriva the third.

Aquinas, as was his custom, summarizes the interpretive tradition as he makes his conclusion. Citing the Church Fathers Origen and Jerome, he says that Joseph

> … did not suspect adultery. For Joseph knew the modesty of Mary: he had read in Scripture that "a Virgin [*virgo*] shall conceive," and "a shoot [*virga*] shall come forth from the root of Jesse, and a flower from his root shall come up": he knew, moreover, that Mary was descended from the line of David; thus he more easily believed that this had been fulfilled in her, than that she had committed fornication. And so believing himself unworthy to live with such holiness, he wished to dismiss her quietly, as Peter says, "Depart from me, Lord, because I am a sinful man." Thus he did not wish to dishonor her—that is, to lead her to himself—and take her in marriage, believing himself unworthy; or, according to others' opinion, not knowing the

end, lest he be found guilty, so to speak, if he kept
the secret and remained with her.[28]

The Catholic Church takes no official position on the
interpretation of the brief passage in St. Matthew's Gospel;
and Christians are free to believe as they wish. The author of
this book finds the reverence theory most persuasive.

St. Luke's Gospel informs us that Mary's time of delivery coincided with an enrollment—a census—of "all the world" (Lk
2:1). In ancient times, as today, a census was a common, useful
tool for the purposes of taxation and the allotment of public
services. There were, however, no mechanical means of record
collection, transfer, or retrieval; so the process could stretch
on for many years.

A census usually took place in two phases. In the first,
there would be a registration of land and property ownership.
In the second, there would be the assignment of payments.[29]
St. Luke associates this particular census with Quirinius, who
was a military commander in the region as early as 9 BC. In 6
AD, the same Quirinius was governor in Syria and still over-
seeing the census.

---

28   St. Thomas Aquinas, *Super Evangelium Matthaei*, Lectio IV, new translation.
29   See Joseph Ratzinger, *Jesus of Nazareth: The Infancy Narratives* (New York:
     Image, 2012), 62–63.

It seems likely that Mary and Joseph made their journey during the first phase of the census. St. Luke suggests that citizens of the Judean kingdom were to be registered according to their ancestry; and so Joseph and Mary, as descendants of David, were required to go to David's city, Bethlehem. One modern commentator believes the requirement applied only to property owners, and so concludes that Joseph must have owned real estate in Bethlehem.[30]

Whatever the reason for their going, it was a difficult journey to make so late in a pregnancy. Yet it brought about the conditions necessary for the fulfillment of Israel's expectation:

> But you, O Bethlehem Eph'rathah, who are little to be among the clans of Judah, from you shall come forth for me one who is to be ruler in Israel, whose origin is from of old, from ancient days. (Mi 5:2; see also Jn 7:42)

And so it was that the child Jesus was born, "seemingly by chance, in the place of the promise."[31]

---

30   Ratzinger, 62–63.
31   Ratzinger, 58.

What was promising for Israel, however, felt threatening to King Herod. The arrival of Jesus coincided with the nadir of Herod's physical and mental health.

It is one of the quirks of written history that we must mark that date of Jesus' birth in years "Before Christ" (BC). Our system of chronology was developed in the sixth century AD by a monk named Denis the Little (Dionysius Exiguus), but Denis miscalculated by several years. Most scholars today place the birth of Jesus somewhere in the range of 7 BC to 4 BC. And Herod died in 4 BC.

But the despot Herod did not go gentle into that good night. His final years were his maddest. As his health declined, he arranged the massacre of three hundred of his military leaders. At the same time, he ordered the execution of one of his sons. In response to an act of vandalism, he had two rabbis burned alive; and then he commanded that all their disciples be found and killed.

Furious with resentment toward all his subjects, he knew that they would celebrate at his death—that not a soul in his kingdom would grieve his passing. *After all he had done for them!* But he was determined to have the last laugh. So he ordered that the most respected men should be rounded up from every village in the land; and he had the lot of them housed at a racetrack. Then he summoned his sister and her husband and told them:

I know well enough that the Jews will keep a
festival upon my death. However, it is in my power
to be mourned on other accounts, and to have a
splendid funeral, if you will but be subservient
to my commands. Take care to send soldiers to
encompass these men that are now in custody, and
slay them immediately upon my death, and then
all Judea, and every family of them, will weep at it,
whether they want to or not.[32] (The executions were
not carried out.)

This was the Herod who received at court the "wise men
from the East," the magi looking for the newborn king of the
Jews (Mt 2:1–2). The description in St. Matthew's Gospel is
fascinating. For it shows that, even in the depths of madness,
Herod retained his diplomatic skills. Recognizing that the
magi were the detectives most likely to locate the child, he
sent them off as his agents. "Go and search diligently for the
child," he said, "and when you have found him bring me word,
that I too may come and worship him" (Mt 2:8). Wise as they
were, they must have been fooled; they decided not to comply
only because they had been warned in a dream (Mt 2:12).

The king, then, proceeded to his usual next step.

Then Herod, when he saw that he had been tricked
by the wise men, was in a furious rage, and he sent

---

and killed all the male children in Bethlehem and
in all that region who were two years old or under,
according to the time which he had ascertained
from the wise men.

—Mt 2:16

In the rolls of Herod's massacres, this one does not rank
high. The historian Josephus did not even judge it worth mentioning. Scholars estimate that fewer than twenty children in
the region would have fit the wise men's description.[33] In the
last years of Herod, a cluster of seven murders was hardly
remarkable. For Herod the Great, it was a slow day.

Throughout these many ordeals, Joseph made prudent
decisions with the guidance of angels—but that bare fact
demands a chapter all its own.

---

33   See, for example, A.E. Harvey, *A Companion to the New Testament*, second
     edition (Cambridge, UK: Cambridge University Press, 2004), 17, and
     Raymond E. Brown et al., *The New Jerome Biblical Commentary* (Englewood
     Cliffs, NJ: Prentice Hall, 1990).

CHAPTER 5
JOSEPH AND HIS ANGELS

The great difficulty in sketching the character of Joseph of Nazareth is that Scripture never shows him speaking. He never says yes or no. He never makes a nod or gesture. And not only is he never shown to speak, the Gospels never show a single human being speaking *to* him—not even his wife or son.

No *humans* speak to him; but four times, an angel speaks to him.

Christian tradition makes much of Mary's Annunciation. The Church commemorates it by a feast day and dedicates a daily prayer to it (the Angelus). But Joseph's "annunciations" are also worthy of scrutiny—certainly for what they reveal about him, but also for what they reveal about angels. The

Gospels present almost every episode in Joseph's life as an encounter with an angel.

The first occurred shortly after he discovered that Mary was pregnant, and he knew that he could not be the baby's father. After what must have been an anguished time—whether it was hours or days, we do not know—he decided to divorce her quietly. When he finally fell asleep, after deliberation and prayer, he must have been exhausted.

> But as he considered this, behold, an angel of the
> Lord appeared to him in a dream, saying, "Joseph,
> son of David, do not fear to take Mary your wife, for
> that which is conceived in her is of the Holy Spirit;
> she will bear a son, and you shall call his name
> Jesus, for he will save his people from their sins."
> —Mt 1:20–21

An angel gave Joseph information he could not otherwise have figured out, and gave him clear instruction about what he was to do. He was to go ahead with the marriage—and stay in the marriage. He was to name the child *not* according to any of the customs of his time. The baby would *not* be named for his father or grandfather, but rather for his mission. He would be called Jesus, *Yeshua*, which means "God is salvation." It was Joseph's right to name the child, but it was an angel who delivered the right name to Joseph.

This was no small contribution. Every Christian through-out history has owed that angel an incalculable debt. For every time Christians have called upon Jesus in prayer, they called upon a name revealed by the angel.

The angel made his second appearance to Joseph after the child was born.

> Now when [the Wise Men] had departed, behold, an angel of the Lord appeared to Joseph in a dream and said, "Rise, take the child and his mother, and flee to Egypt, and remain there till I tell you; for Herod is about to search for the child, to destroy him."
> —Mt 2:13

This second appearance is significant for many reasons. It shows once again that the angel served Joseph as a guide, but also as a guardian. Joseph received heavenly help in figuring out what to do next, but he also got a stern warning about what he must avoid and flee.

The angel told Joseph that the most powerful man in his world, the mad and cruel King Herod, was targeting the baby Jesus for destruction. Herod had an army at his disposal. He had absolute authority over every little village or desert spot where Joseph might try to hide. Massacres were a hallmark of Herod's reign. So this was serious business. And how else could a man like Joseph have discovered the danger? He was a carpenter, a commoner, and he did not frequent the parties in Herod's palace. He did not have friends at court.

But heaven made sure that Joseph was at no disadvantage. In his second visit from an angel, Joseph was told what to do and where to go. And he acted promptly. After this apparition, he moved his family immediately to Egypt.

The third angelic visit to Joseph came one or two years later. Here is how St. Matthew tells it.

> But when Herod died, behold, an angel of the Lord appeared in a dream to Joseph in Egypt, saying, "Rise, take the child and his mother, and go to the land of Israel, for those who sought the child's life are dead."
> —Mt 2:19–20

Here again, the angel appeared as guardian and guide, bringing the Holy Family safely home to the Holy Land because the Holy Land was waiting for its messiah, its deliverer and redeemer. And the task of this third angel-visit continued in the fourth angel-visit, which occurred while Joseph was leading the family on their return journey.

> But when [Joseph] heard that Archela'us reigned over Judea in place of his father Herod, he was afraid to go there, and being warned in a dream he withdrew to the district of Galilee.
> —Mt 2:22

One last time, the Holy Family eluded danger, thanks to a warning from Joseph's angel—a warning given in a dream.

Those few scenes are important because they tell us almost everything we know about the man whom God chose to watch over his only Son. They tell us almost everything we know about the hero the Gospel praises as a "just man"—which is the highest compliment you could receive in first-century Jewish society. They tell us almost everything we know about Joseph.

And what we know about this silent man is that he was intensely devoted to the angels. He listened to them. He followed through on their instructions.

By the time he had reached adulthood, he was accustomed to their promptings. Nowhere do the Gospels register his surprise at the appearance of an angel. He shows none of the fright that we see in the stories of prophets like Balaam (Nm 22:31–34) and Daniel (Dn 10:5–9). Both of those men dropped to the ground in fear; Daniel even fell unconscious.

But like the prophets, Joseph was open to the counsel of the angels. Even when he had firmly decided upon a course of action, he was willing to drop all his plans suddenly, simply because of the prompting of his angel. This calm readiness is impressive, and it's unusual among even the heroes in Israel's history. It surely speaks volumes about Joseph's previous habits of prayer.

For devotion to the angels was common in his time. We see this in much of the New Testament: the Gospels, the Acts of the Apostles, the Epistles, and especially the Book of Revelation. St. Luke speaks of the general importance of the angels by letting us know that the Sadducees were the *only* Jews of his time who did *not* believe in angels (see Acts 23:8).

Even outside the Bible, however, there is abundant evidence for ancient Israel's devotion to the angels. It is everywhere, for example, in the Dead Sea Scrolls. The Scrolls are a library of documents discovered in the mid-twentieth century in the Judean desert, near the site of an ancient Essene community. Many of them date to the lifetime of Joseph and Mary. They seem to indicate that the Essene movement was much preoccupied with the heavenly spirits. The sect that produced the Scrolls was preparing for a world war in which they would fight in alliance with angelic armies. Together, heaven and earth would make war for the recovery of the Holy Land and the restoration of God's law. To that end, the Essenes were required to memorize the names of the angels.

When they worshipped, they believed that they were worshipping together with invisible, innumerable hosts. (Catholics still believe this, today.) They looked especially to the help of the Archangel Michael (again, as Catholics still do, today). The *War Scroll* reassures its readers:

But, as for you, take courage and do not fear.... Israel is all that is and that will be.... Today is his appointed time to subdue and to humiliate the prince of the realm of wickedness. He will send eternal support to the company of his redeemed by the power of the majestic angel of the authority of Michael. By eternal light he shall joyfully light up the covenant of Israel—peace and blessing for the lot of God—to exalt the authority of Michael among the gods and the dominion of Israel among all flesh.[34]

Angels were also very important to the first-century Jewish philosopher Philo of Alexandria. In fact, Philo spoke at length about why and how God sent some people visions in dreams. The archetype of this, for Philo, was the Patriarch Jacob, who dreamt of the ladder of angels reaching to heaven.[35]

Devotion to the angels was important to many of the Jewish authors whose works have survived from antiquity. It stood in continuity with the Scriptures Joseph heard in the synagogue of Nazareth.

The book of Genesis begins with the creation of "the heavens," which are understood to be the spiritual realm, and the

---

34 1QM 17.4-8 (Qumran War Scroll), in Michael Wise, Martin Abegg, Jr., and Edward Cook, *The Dead Sea Scrolls: A New Translation* (San Francisco: Harper, 1996), 165.

35 Philo, *On Dreams: That They Are God-Sent*, 1.1.

"lights," which is a name Scripture uses elsewhere to denote the angels. The serpent that tempts Adam and Eve is a fallen angel; and when God expels the primal couple, he sets other pure spirits, cherubim, as guards of the garden sanctuary (Gn 3:24).

The presence of the angels continues in the time of the patriarchs. An angel stayed the hand of Abraham when he went to Mount Moriah to sacrifice Isaac his son (Gn 22:11–12). The patriarch Jacob wrestled with an angel (Gn 32:24–25) and fought alongside an army of angels (Gn 32:1–2). And one day he rested his head on a stone—"And he dreamed that there was a ladder set up on the earth, and the top of it reached to heaven; and behold, the angels of God were ascending and descending on it!" (Gn 28:12).

Angels were everywhere in the Hebrew Scriptures. They were in the Law, the Prophets, the Psalms, and the Writings. They were mentioned in the rituals celebrated on feast days at the temple. They abounded in the popular devotions of ordinary Jews.

So Joseph lived, as his forebears had lived, in a world saturated with angels. Because he was devout—because he was a just man—he followed the religious traditions of his ancestors. He attended the customary services. He said the prayers that he had been taught. And because of these habits, he was alert to the angels' presence and activity. He knew their company and their help.

CNO

Modern readers have a tendency to reduce the lives of biblical figures to the scenes that are preserved in Scripture. If we do this with Joseph, however, and we reduce him to just those few scenes with angels, we might conclude that he was indeed an unusual man. We might think his life was like an action movie, but with even less talk and more special effects. He was always, it seems, in the midst of danger, or high drama, or distant travel, or deep adventure.

And those wild episodes were surely definitive for his life. Nevertheless, they probably occupied just a few days in total. And he was married for thousands of days.

Unfortunately, the Gospels don't give any close-ups of his ordinary days. Tradition refers to those days as the "hidden life" of the Holy Family.

Yet the Gospels don't leave posterity entirely in the dark. What the Evangelists reveal is that Joseph's reputation did not rest on his adventures. So, apparently, he did not talk much about them.

When his neighbors thought about him at all, they referred to him simply as "the carpenter"—not the man who traveled to Egypt—not the man who was visited by Persian Magi—not the mortal enemy of the loathsome Herod. He was simply "the carpenter"; and Jesus was simply the carpenter's son.

He was known for his work, and his work was not biblical interpretation, or preaching, or teaching, or philosophy, or theology. He wasn't a thinker like Philo of Alexandria. He wasn't a priest like Mary's kinsman Zechariah.

Though God had chosen Joseph for the greatest mission ever, he was an ordinary workingman. And this is a supremely important fact: he was no less ordinary for the fact that he was close to the angels.

Why is this fact so important? Because in the midst of every believer's daily work, the angels are there; God wants everyone to be close to the angels, attentive to the angels, and alert to their promptings. This is not a gift or a skill for unusual people. This is for everyone, as it was for Joseph.

What was his work like in the day-to-day?

From childhood onward, Joseph probably worked with crews of men. They commuted together to sites by walking, perhaps for miles. Their work was demanding on both muscle and mind. Their worksites were noisy with the sound of hammers and saws and voices. Many of Joseph's co-workers were probably rough and uncouth.

Yet *in the midst of all that racket* Joseph cultivated interior silence and the habit of prayer.

&

Theologians in later times often referred to Joseph as "the Angelic Man." They did this for two reasons. First of all, and obviously, because he had at least four vivid encounters with angels in his lifetime. That is four more, perhaps, than most people have. But there is another reason why he was "angelic." He was angelic, the theologians say, because he received in abundance the particular gifts of all the pure spirits in heaven.

This argument is developed most fully in the work of Jerónimo Gracián, a sixteenth-century Carmelite friar, best known as the spiritual director of St. Teresa of Avila.[36]

Gracián follows the Christian interpretive tradition, which identifies in the Bible nine distinct orders (or *choirs*) of pure spirits in heaven. There are angels, archangels, and principalities; virtues, powers, and dominions; and thrones, cherubim, and seraphim. Each grouping has its particular way of serving God—a particular, "angelic" way. And yet, Gracián says, Joseph managed to fulfill the requirements of each and every group.

An angel, in the biblical languages, is simply a "messenger." That is the literal meaning of the Hebrew *malakh* and Greek *angelos*. Even as they delivered messages, however, the angels commonly served also as guardians and guides (see, for

---

36   The reflection that follows is loosely based on Fr. Joseph Chorpenning's remarkable edition of Gracián's work, *Just Man, Husband of Mary, Guardian of Christ: An Anthology from Jerónimo Gracián's Summary of the Excellencies of St. Joseph (1597)* (Philadelphia: St. Joseph's University Press, 1993), especially pages 187–200.

example, Gn 16:7–13 and Zec 1:8–21). Like the angels, Joseph served as a messenger between heaven and the Holy Family, and then served as the family's guide and protector.

An archangel is a ruling angel. To archangels, in the Scriptures, God assigns the tasks of greatest gravity. The only spirit identified in the Bible as an archangel is Michael, who consistently opposes the devil in direct combat (see Jude 9, Rv 12:7). In the interpretive tradition, Gabriel (Lk 1:26) and Raphael (Tb 12:15) are also identified as archangels. St. Paul reveals that an archangel will announce the resurrection of the dead at the end of time (1 Thes 4:16). Like these ruling angels, Joseph was given a task of utmost gravity; his combat required direct engagement with evil; and he bore messages to Jesus and Mary.

The principalities are God's ordinary and immediate servants in the concerns of the visible world. Some scholars identify them with the guardian spirits of nations (see Sir 17:17). St. Paul mentions the principalities often (see Rom 8:38, Eph 3:10; Colossians 1:16); he speaks of some of them among the malicious spirits (see Eph 6:12; Col 2:15). According to the later Church Fathers, the principalities have a special concern for the leaders of nations and leaders in religion.[37] After the manner of the principalities, Joseph was given authority over the household of the Holy Family—and special care for the King of Kings.

---

37   See Dionysius the Areopagite, *Celestial Hierarchy*, 9.1-2.

The powers are those spirits specially commissioned to restrain evil spirits and punish them. St. Paul usually speaks of them together with the principalities (see above) and in the same way. Like the heavenly powers, Joseph manifested God's strength through his defeat of King Herod the Great. He was able to maintain a holy life and household even in Egypt, a land proverbial for its idolatry and magic.

The virtues are the spirits through whom God performs astonishing works and great miracles—for example, Joshua's stilling of the sun and moon (Jos 10:12–13). According to tradition, Satan was created in this order, and since his fall he depends upon empty spectacle—a parody of the miracles for which he was created. Like the good virtues, Joseph of Nazareth mediated God's miracles on earth through the ministry of his Son, Jesus. It was Joseph who raised the world's greatest miracle-worker.

The dominions (sometimes rendered "dominations") are assigned to the regulation of other pure spirits. St. Paul mentions them in Colossians 1:16. By their ordinary service they demonstrate the necessity of hierarchy in every social order, even in heaven. Like these spirits, Joseph held true authority. Even God himself—in the person of Jesus—submitted to Joseph's dominion and was obedient to him (see Lk 2:51).

The thrones in heaven represent the agents of God's rule, justice, and judgment. They are alive, and the prophet Daniel represents them as fire (Dn 7:9), and Ezekiel as a sapphire that is brilliant and clear (Ez 10:1). In Bethlehem, Nazareth, and Egypt, Joseph was like the thrones in heaven: he upheld almighty God as he cradled Jesus in his arms.

The cherubim appear often in the Bible, and they are usually associated with close proximity to God. When God expelled Adam and Eve from the Garden of Eden, he placed cherubim as guards, with flaming swords, in order to keep the primal couple away. After the Exodus, God commanded the Israelites to place golden images of the cherubim on the ark of the covenant (Ex 25:18–22). He ordered them also to embroider cherubim into the curtains and veils of the tabernacle (Ex 26:1, 31). For the inner sanctuary of the Jerusalem temple (the Holy of Holies), Solomon fashioned two gigantic cherubim out of olive wood—each one fifteen feet tall and plated with gold (1 Kgs 6:23–25). Joseph, like the cherubim, spent his days closely contemplating the Almighty—God incarnate in Jesus Christ. As the cherubim flanked the seat of God on the ark, so Joseph and Mary flanked the earthly throne of the King of Kings.

The seraphim are the highest attendants in the court of God. Their name in Hebrew means "fiery ones," and it describes their great love. They appear only once in Scripture, in the prophet Isaiah's vision of heaven's throne (Is 6:2–6); but they are mentioned also in apocryphal literature that was popular in Joseph's lifetime.[38] It is the seraphim who perpetually

---

38   See, for example, the *First Book of Enoch*, 61.10 and 71.7.

sing the hymn "Holy, Holy, Holy" to God in heaven (Is 6:3; Rv 4:8). Like the seraphim, Joseph burned with an ardent love as he lived in the earthly court of Almighty God; and "holy" is the name given by tradition to Joseph's family.

By comparing Joseph to each of the ranks of pure spirits, Jerónimo Gracián justifies the title "Angelic Man" for Joseph of Nazareth. Joseph surpassed all the orders of heaven in his excellence. He was nearer to God and served him more closely and constantly than even the angels . For this reason, Joseph received such close attention from the angels. In heaven he was already seen as a prince.

Yet he was no less ordinary for all that. He was no less a workingman. He was no less and no more than "the carpenter."

Gracián's analysis has implications not only for Joseph's life, but also for the lives of Christians in every generation. Through baptism, all believers have been given a place in the divine household and have been called to share a table with Mary and Joseph and Jesus.

Like Joseph, all Christians are now able to serve Jesus in close proximity—as close as the angels—and as constantly as Joseph served him. Work need not be an interruption of love, and in most cases it is not. For dedicated parents, work is often an expression of love. In Joseph's work he loved his wife and son, even when his work took him away from home, even when his work required his most intense concentration, and even when he was working in Egypt's blistering summer heat.

Like Joseph, all Christians can be "angelic" as they bear Jesus sacramentally and carry his presence out into the world—a world that still has its Herods, hostile to the Lord.

God calls ordinary believers, as he called Joseph, to be his messengers and guardians, his power and his voice. He calls ordinary believers to be contemplatives in the middle of their neighborhoods and workplaces.

Father Gracián takes his reflection a step further. He notes that theologians, long before the sixteenth century, had debated the question of whether Jesus had a guardian angel—and many concluded that he did not.[39]

Gracián revisited their arguments and concluded that they were half-right. Jesus had no guardian from heaven, he argued, but God chose Joseph himself to be Jesus' guardian "angel." Again, this is the speculation of theologians, not Catholic doctrine. But it is a remarkable argument to consider.

Joseph was given no more in life than most ordinary people. In fact, by modern material standards, he had very little. He had skills, and he had a job. He had what he needed to get by. But God did not call him to get by. God entrusted his helpless baby son to Joseph's care. And then he let Joseph know

---

39   Chorpenning, 190–191.

that a mighty king and his army wanted the boy dead. In fact, *all the powers of hell* were arrayed for the downfall of that son.

Then God sent word that Joseph would have to undertake a long trip, in haste, into a hostile land, where people might not speak his language or respect his customs.

The unspoken word behind God's call is *trust*. Joseph was called to remember the marvels of the Lord—to remember the divine acts that were proclaimed in synagogue and temple and at home—and trust the Lord who had worked those marvels.

CHAPTER 6
FLIGHT FROM HEROD

The warning came in a dream: "Rise, take the child and his mother, and flee to Egypt, and remain there till I tell you; for Herod is about to search for the child, to destroy him" (Mt 2:13). Joseph had been asleep. It was late in the night, and even the roads in town were barely navigable for the darkness. Beyond the town, there was not a glimmer of light.

They had no time to prepare. Packing for maximum speed, they could carry few possessions with them. They would have to make the journey with little more than the clothes they wore and the divine baby in their arms.

This could not be delayed till morning. Mary and Joseph had spent the whole of their lives in a land ruled by Herod. They knew no other world. They had never seen another world. They knew that Herod would act swiftly, decisively, and effectively. Every despot in the Mediterranean region was capable of murderous cruelty. The Persians were notorious for it; and the Romans were every bit their equal. History showed that the Hasmoneans, too, had been inclined to slaughter and exemplary public torture. But Herod was efficient, and he did not allow himself or his forces to fail.

In richly symbolic language, the Book of Revelation conveys the stress of the Holy Family's flight:

> [The dragon's] tail swept down a third of the stars of heaven, and cast them to the earth. And the dragon stood before the woman who was about to bear a child, that he might devour her child when she brought it forth; she brought forth a male child, one who is to rule all the nations with a rod of iron, but her child was caught up to God and to his throne, and the woman fled into the wilderness, where she has a place prepared by God, in which to be nourished for one thousand two hundred and sixty days.
> —Rv 12:4–6

The narrative is complex. It is clear that the dragon refers, at one level, to Herod the Great, who sought the death of the "male child ... who is to rule all the nations."[40] Yet it refers also

---

40   On the identification of the apocalyptic dragon with Herod and his dynasty, see George Wesley Buchanan, *The Book of Revelation: Its Introduction and Prophecy* (Eugene, OR: Wipf and Stock, 2005), 348–362. See also the fifth-century *Vision of Theophilus*, Book 3.

to some other, superhuman power that is perpetually opposed to the child, the woman, and their family (Rv 12:13, 17). The passage harks back to Eden, where the serpent warred against Adam and Eve; and it evokes the incident of Israel's sons selling Joseph into Egyptian slavery. It may anticipate later events, too, such as the years-long siege of Jerusalem.

All the drama of history seems to be concentrated into that moment—that night when Joseph awoke from his encounter with the angel. If the whole family could not perceive the matter in its totality, they certainly could feel their immediate peril. Such feelings pass unspoken between husband and wife, especially those who have known one another since childhood. And emotions pass from mother to child in the milk of the breast.

The passage from the Apocalypse begins in darkness, with even the stars put out of the sky. Joseph must have felt and feared the enveloping night.

It was no shame to feel fear. To be fearless in such a time is to be truly mad. Fear is the instinctive human response to bodily danger. In a father, it triggers the actions that will preserve his family and himself. Fortitude means not a lack of fear, but a right ordering of fears. Joseph feared the possibility of failing God far more than he feared the wrath of Herod. And he feared the loss of his son more than the loss of his own life.

☙❧

The German scholar Oscar Meinardus spent years attempting to reconstruct the Holy Family's flight to Egypt. He drew from the Gospels, but also from archaeology, ancient papyri discovered in modern times, and the oral traditions of Egypt's Christians, the Copts. He gathered his results in a book-length study, which he revised repeatedly through decades of research.[41]

Even today, pilgrims in Egypt follow a trail of sites—monasteries, shrines, and churches, built at places where Joseph and his family allegedly stopped for rest or longer refuge. In 2001, the American journalist Paul Perry followed this trail in a two-month tour he later detailed in a book and documentary film. He explored more than thirty sites.[42]

These itineraries cannot be verified by scientific means; but they surely represent the scale of the Holy Family's trip. No matter which route Joseph took, he had to travel the better part of a thousand miles, with a wife who was recently postpartum and their infant child.

Most of the reconstructions follow roughly the same route. Scripture records that the family visited Jerusalem forty days after Jesus' birth for Mary's ritual purification and Jesus'

41   See Otto F.A. Meinardus, *In the Steps of the Holy Family: From Bethlehem to Upper Egypt* (Cairo: Dar Al-Maaref, 1963); *The Holy Family in Egypt* (Cairo: American University in Cairo Press, 1986); and *Two Thousand Years of Coptic Christianity* (Cairo: American University in Cairo Press, 1999), 14 –27.

42   Paul Perry, *Jesus in Egypt: Discovering the Secrets of Christ's Childhood Years* (New York: Ballantine, 2003).

presentation in the temple (Lk 2:22–38). Afterward, "they returned into Galilee, to their own city, Nazareth" (Lk 2:39).

It seems that the warning must have arrived while they were home among their people. Joseph would have left with a route in mind. From business travel, he knew the roads. He knew the construction sites. He knew the synagogues along the way that welcomed travelers for safe sleeping. In his plans, he must have considered possible stopping places within his and Mary's social networks. They could perhaps stay with other members of the House of David, or sympathetic members of the Essene movement. The journey would take weeks (at least) of nighttime travel and daytime hiding. And in any town or village they might encounter Herod's spies. Surely, too, they were wary of endangering friends and family.

It would be impossible to sort out all the problems before leaving Bethlehem. They could only sketch possibilities. The rest they would have to leave to God.

From Bethlehem the Holy Family would have traveled westward toward the Mediterranean coast, and then southward along the coast for a hundred miles to Gaza. From Gaza they would have gone on to cross the Jordan River into the country of the Nabateans. There, among the Gentiles, the refugees would have found some degree of safety. The Nabatean rulers were quarreling with Herod at the time—and strongly resisting his efforts to absorb them into his kingdom.

Beyond the lands ruled by Herod, the family could travel by day. They passed through cities and villages and desert wastes. They continued westward through Nabatea until they came to the border, the tiny "River of Egypt," which they crossed, and entered the land that would be their refuge.

The reports of the Holy Family's movements afterward are scattered and contradictory. Most agree that they traveled to the interior of Egypt and then south along the big river, the River Nile.

There were enclaves of Jews throughout Nabatea and Egypt, and there were synagogues. So it is likely that the Holy Family found hospitality along their route.

In Egypt, Jews represented around four percent of the population—about the same proportion they have in the United States today.[43] Jews served at the Egyptian royal court and in the high ranks of the military. In this land where they had once been enslaved, they were now enjoying a revival in Jewish literary culture. There were many synagogues, in cities and towns, and thriving neighborhoods where Jewish feasts and customs were faithfully observed. The city of Alexandria had a large Jewish population that occupied two sizable neighborhoods by the seashore. There were even suburbs and distant exurbs known as "villages of the Jews."[44]

---

43   Joseph Mélèze Modrzejewski, *The Jews of Egypt: From Ramses II to Emperor Hadrian* (Princeton, NJ: Princeton University Press, 1995), 74.

44   Victor Tcherikover, *Hellenistic Civilization and the Jews* (New York: Atheneum, 1982), 284–285.

In Egypt, the Hebrew Scriptures had been rendered in a brilliant Greek translation, known as the Septuagint. Some Jewish families were well established in the country and quite well off. Their stately tombs have survived for millennia; their mansions must have been grandiose. The Romans, under Augustus, had accommodated Jewish practice and exempted them from certain taxes.

A half-century later, the Jewish philosopher Philo could thrive in the old Egyptian city of Alexandria. He even testified to the presence of a sect in Alexandria, the Therapeutae, who bore a strong resemblance to the Essenes. The names "Essene" and "Therapeutae" both mean "healers." Many modern scholars, in fact, believe that the Therapeutae were simply the Greek-speaking Egyptian community of Essenes.[45]

The surrounding culture could be hostile. The Jews of Egypt met sporadic and sometimes vicious discrimination at the hands of their Greek-speaking neighbors and rulers. They were sometimes resented for their successes and envied for the favors they received from Rome. Jewish riots were not uncommon, and neither were anti-Jewish riots. The ancient garbage dumps preserve the paperwork from many lawsuits in which Jews petitioned for their rights.[46]

---

45   See, for example, Kaufmann Kohler, "Therapeutae," *Jewish Encyclopedia*, JewishEncyclopedia.com/articles/14366-therapeutae (accessed March 1, 2020).

46   See John M.G. Barclay, *Jews in the Mediterranean Diaspora: From Alexander to Trajan* (Edinburgh: T&T Clark, 1996), 48–51.

Nevertheless, in Egypt, Joseph's family could breathe with relative ease. Joseph would likely find a place for them among their own people—a safe place where they could raise their son in the ways of their ancestors. Moreover, he could find work among people who shared his traditions. It is likely that, from professional experience, he could already speak the common Greek language with some degree of fluency.

Home was so far away; but, for refugees in flight, after weeks of running, stability and safety can feel a lot like home.

The New Testament records no details of the Holy Family's time in Egypt. There is no certain record of how long they stayed. Some commentators believe the "one thousand two hundred and sixty days" of Revelation 12:6 is an exact accounting of their sojourn. Other ancient commentators preserve other traditions. Scripture suggests, however, that the Holy Family's exile came to an end with the death of Herod the Great in 4 BC.

The news would have quickly reached the Jewish community in Egypt—probably within a few days of the event. Joseph probably knew instantly, however, because his news came from an angel. The account in St. Matthew's Gospel gives the impression that Joseph immediately packed up his family and headed in the direction of home.

> But when Herod died, behold, an angel of the Lord
> appeared in a dream to Joseph in Egypt, saying,
> "Rise, take the child and his mother, and go to the

land of Israel, for those who sought the child's life
are dead." And he rose and took the child and his
mother, and went to the land of Israel.

—Mt 2:19–21

The Holy Family's return would have been as physically
challenging as the flight to Egypt had been. All travel in antiquity was arduous. The roads were pocked and perilous for
people and beasts. The roadsides were prowled by gangs of
thieves. Lodging along the way was often filthy and had its
own perils.

But on this voyage, they were spared the stress of Herod's
pursuit. Along the way, they probably received the news that
Caesar Augustus had acted to weaken the Jewish kingdom by
dividing it into four territories, three to be ruled by Herod's
sons and one by his sister. Joseph had to make a judgment
call: Which of these heirs posed the least threat and which
the greatest? He chose to take up residence in Galilee, where
there were other small Davidic settlements. St. Matthew's
Gospel says: "But when he heard that Archelaus reigned over
Judea in place of his father Herod, he was afraid to go there,
and being warned in a dream he withdrew to the district of
Galilee" (Mt 2:22).

Christians have always been curious about the Holy Family's time in Egypt, and writers from the second century to
the twentieth have produced fiction imagining it as a time
of miracles. In ancient "Infancy Gospels" the toddler Jesus

breathes on his toys to make them come alive; and he visits severe judgment on neighborhood bullies. The New Testament apocrypha present a character who has nothing in common with the Jesus of history—the Jesus of the Gospels.

What can we know for certain about the Holy Family's days abroad? It seems likely that in Egypt, Jesus caught his first glimpses of his father, Joseph, at work.

CHAPTER 7
JOSEPH AND HIS WORK

He was a silent man. And one of his titles in modern devotion draws further attention to his silence: St. Joseph *the Worker*. The Catholic Church remembers St. John of Antioch as "Golden Mouth" (Chrysostom) and St. Peter of Ravenna for his "Golden Words" (Chrysologus). But we remember Joseph for getting things done. Among all who have labored, in all of human history, he is the one known as "the Worker."

In the Gospels, Joseph's identity is bound up with his relationships and his labor. He is the son of Jacob. He is the husband of Mary. He is the earthly father of Jesus. He is the companion of angels.

He is a son, a husband, a father. And he is a *tekton*—a craftsman, an artisan. An ancient tradition tells us more specifically that his craft was carpentry, a trade in which he apprenticed his son Jesus. When people were astonished at Jesus' teaching, they asked: "Is not this the carpenter's son?" (Mt 13:55).

And all of this is fitting. In the fourth century, St. Ambrose wrote, "It does not seem strange to declare that Jesus had a craftsman for a father. By this sign, he effectively showed us that he had the Craftsman of all things for a Father."[47] Later spiritual writers pointed out that Jesus' earthly father shared two titles with Jesus' heavenly Father. Both Joseph and God are called "Father," and both are called "Craftsman." In working, Joseph knew that he was godlike; and he knew this not because of an angel's message, but because he had heard the Scriptures proclaimed in synagogue. What Joseph knew about work—like what he knew about the angels—he had learned from the first pages of the Book of Genesis.

Pope Francis gave a modern voice to this ancient understanding. He said:

It is clear from the very first pages of the Bible that work is an essential part of human dignity; there we read that "the Lord God took the man and put him in the garden of Eden to till it and keep it" (Gn 2:15). Man is presented as a laborer who works the earth, harnesses the forces of nature and produces

---

47   St. Ambrose of Milan, *Exposition on the Gospel of St. Luke*, 3.1.

"the bread of anxious toil" (Ps 127:2), in addition to cultivating his own gifts and talents.[48]

This papal statement harks back to the beginning, to the story of Adam and Eve, which Joseph knew well. He knew it from the liturgy in the synagogue and the temple—and he allowed it to shape his life and his approach to his craft. And because he did this, he became not only a builder of benches and tables. Like Adam and like God, he became a builder of the world.

Those first pages of the Bible declare that man was made in God's image (Gn 1:26–27). The very next lines say that he was made *to work*—to have dominion over all the creatures of the earth, sea, and sky. Immediately upon creation, man was given a task. He was told to "fill the earth and subdue it" (Gn 1:28, also 26). He was told to work.

In the chapter that follows, the Book of Genesis examines the same story up close, so to speak, and in slow motion. It is the same story, but told in terms of human drama rather than divine action. In Genesis, chapter two, the reader discovers that the Lord God placed man "in the garden of Eden to till it and keep it" (Gn 2:15). Again, the message is clear: Adam was

---

48   Francis, Apostolic Exhortation *Amoris Laetitia* (March 19, 2016), 23.

created from the earth in order to rule the earth by working the earth.

All the days of work, furthermore, were ordered to leisure on the seventh day. All labor was ordered to rest in worship. So runs the commandment in Exodus:

> Six days you shall labor, and do all your work, … for in six days the LORD made heaven and earth, the sea, and all that is in them, and rested the seventh day; therefore the LORD blessed the Sabbath day and hallowed it. (Ex 20:9,11)

Thus, human beings were created in God's image with labor as a basic part of their nature. The daily rhythm of life was the rhythm of work, and all work was directed back to God, in the end, in worship.

For Israel, the meaning of work was overwhelmingly positive. In his study of the spirituality of work, Archbishop José Gómez noted the preponderance of laborers among the heroes of the Hebrew Scriptures.

> The Old Testament mentions dozens of occupations, including doctors, pharmacists, artisans, blacksmiths, scholars, sailors, builders, musicians, shepherds, and more. The great patriarchs of Israel were all identified with their occupations. Abraham was a herdsman, Noah was a farmer, Isaac and

Jacob likewise worked the land. King David was a shepherd.... [W]isdom literature offers opinions on the moral challenges facing merchants and salesmen, in addition to praising manual labor and condemning idleness.[49]

The later rabbis preserved the interpretive tradition as Joseph would likely have heard it in synagogue and at home; and it places a religious premium on crafts and craftsmen. The Babylonian Talmud holds that the "four carpenters" presented in the biblical Book of Zechariah (1:20) were the messiah son of David, the messiah son of Joseph, the prophet Elijah, and the Priest of Righteousness.[50] All these figures were expected to appear (or reappear) prominently in the fullness of time; and all were carpenters! Even in the present life, however— even before the end times—the rabbis believed that diligent labor would draw divine rewards. Again, the Talmud says: "Seven years lasted the famine, but it came not to the artisan's door."[51] Scholar David Fiensy concludes, "The rabbinic sources extol both manual labor and teaching one's son a craft. Artisans often receive special recognition, and many of the sages were artisans."[52]

---

49   José H. Gómez, "All You Who Labor: Towards a Spirituality of Work for the 21st Century," *Notre Dame Journal of Law, Ethics and Public Policy* 20, no. 2 (2006): 791–814.

50   Babylonian Talmud, *Tractate Sukkah*, 5.

51   Babylonian Talmud, *Tractate Sanhedrin*, 3.

52   Fiensy, 240.

In this valuing of craftsmen, the Jews stood alone among ancient peoples.[53] The Greeks disdained manual laborers and tried to minimize their participation in democracy.[54] Socrates held that citizens should come only from the leisured classes—and in fact should be prohibited "to exercise any mechanical craft at all."[55] Aristotle agreed: "Nature," he said,

> would like to distinguish between the bodies of freemen and slaves, making the one strong for servile labor, the other upright, and although useless for such services, useful for political life in the arts both of war and peace.

He also said, "those whose business is to use their body, and who can do nothing better" are "by nature slaves, and it is better for them as for all inferiors that they should be under the rule of a master."[56] It was Aristotle's firm belief that "no man can practice virtue who is living the life of a mechanic or laborer."[57]

The Greek historian Herodotus observed that this attitude toward laborers was universal.

---

53   See the discussion in Paul Veyne, *A History of Private Life: From Pagan Rome to Byzantium* (Cambridge, MA: Harvard University Press, 1987), 117–137. See also Fiensy, 239, 255.

54   See Aristotle, *Politics*, 6.4.

55   Xenophon, *The Economist*, 4.

56   See Aristotle, *Politics*, 1.5.

57   See Aristotle, *Politics*, 3.5.

Now whether this, too, the Greeks have learned
from the Egyptians, I cannot confidently judge. I
know that in Thrace and Scythia and Persia and
Lydia and nearly all foreign countries, those who
learn trades are held in less esteem than the rest
of the people, and those who have least to do with
artisans' work … are highly honored.[58]

Israel, it seems, turned the values of the rest of the world
on their head. The people of Judea esteemed those who worked
with muscle as well as mind. They worshipped a God who
revealed himself to be an artisan, and they honored those who
labored on earth in this godlike way.

As Joseph had grown up in a trade, so he raised his Son, Jesus.
The boy learned his craft at first through proximity—hearing
the conversation of the men while they worked… watching the
way they carried planks and beams and held them in place…
noting the different varieties of nails, bits, and tools.

The work was good. Honest work was always good
because it had been commanded by the Lord and was carried
out in imitation of the Lord. Later generations would fantasize
that work itself was punishment for Adam's fall; but there is

---

58   Herodotus, *History*, 2.167.

no evidence in the Book of Genesis to support that conclusion. The command to work came to Adam in his innocence. After the original sin, he found his work arduous, but it was still good work. The rabbis agreed upon this point.

It was more than good, in fact; it was holy. Biblical scholars note that the command to work, given in Genesis, conferred a primordial priesthood on Adam. God told him "to till [the ground] and keep it" (Gn 2:15). The Hebrew verbs are *abodah* and *shamar*, and they appear together elsewhere in the Bible *only* to describe the sacrificial activity of Israel's priests.[59] Adam's work was supposed to be his offering to God. It was his priestly service. The ground he tilled was his altar, which he was to guard and "keep" from profanation.

Adam, of course, failed in his priestly task; and the Hebrew Scriptures can be read as a history of humanity's efforts to restore legitimate sacrifice on earth. Every effort failed. But the last of the canonical prophets, Malachi, foresaw a day when such sacrifice would take place everywhere:

> from the rising of the sun to its setting my name is great among the nations, and in every place incense is offered to my name, and a pure offering; for my name is great among the nations, says the LORD of hosts. (Mal 1:11)

---

59   See the discussion of these terms in Scott Hahn, *A Father Who Keeps His Promises: God's Covenant Love in Scripture* (Ann Arbor, MI: Servant, 1998), 58–59.

Jesus, in adulthood, would announce the fulfillment of Malachi's oracle in himself (see Jn 4:21–24). St. Paul would confirm that Jesus was the New Adam (see Rom 5:19 and 1 Cor 15:22). In Jesus, the priesthood was restored perfectly; so he, at last, could offer the world in the way Adam should have. All the work that Jesus did—even his first halting effort as a small child—was a pure offering to his heavenly Father.

Joseph shared in that work. He labored in close proximity to Jesus, and he watched as "the child grew and became strong, filled with wisdom" (Lk 2:40). Their work was collaborative, by mutual intention, and the carpenter-father's offering was made perfect at the hand of his carpenter-son.

The writers of the apocryphal gospels, however, get this exactly wrong. They imagine Jesus stretching beams when his father's measurements fell short.[60] But the Lord's offering surely did not fix anyone's professional failings; it sanctified them instead, and even failures can be sanctified. Jesus' own life, as he breathed his last on the cross, had all the appearances of failure, by every earthly measure; and yet it was the supreme success, by every spiritual measure.

The labors in Joseph's workshop were already redemptive, even before our redemption was "finished" (Jn 19:28, 30), and Joseph served as a willing participant, a true concelebrant, just by doing his part and doing it as well as he could.

---

60   See *Infancy Gospel of Thomas*, 13.

We can be sure that Joseph was busy throughout his working life. Herod initiated an unprecedented worldwide building boom, and he left many projects—including the Jerusalem temple—unfinished at the time of his death. His heirs were neither the innovators nor the artists their father had been; but they kept a brisk pace in new construction. The Roman military and commercial presence increased after the death of Herod, as Caesar Augustus divided the kingdom into four "tetrarchies." These social and political changes meant more jobs for the craftsmen in Galilee. As long as Joseph could work, there was work for him to do.

CHAPTER 8

HANDING ON
THE PASSOVER

Joseph was faithful. Though his son was the Messiah—the Son of David and the Son of God—it was clear from his birth that these facts won his family no special treatment on earth. Jesus' life began in extreme hardship. He knew no privilege, and he conferred no social status on his parents.

To some men, this would have been a stumbling block, but not to Joseph. Among the Jews, there was an expectation, based on the oracles of the prophet Isaiah, that the messiah would be "a man of sorrows, and acquainted with grief" (Is 53:3; see also Wis 2:12–20). In Joseph's lifetime, the Essenes were bearers of this "Suffering Servant" tradition. In one of the Thanksgiving Psalms found among the Dead Sea Scrolls, the messiah declares, "Who has been despised like me? And who has been rejected of men like me? And who compares to me in enduring evil?" Yet the same hymn concludes, "Who is like me among the angels."[61] The Essenes expected a redeemer who was scorned and ill-treated, but still superior to the hosts of heaven.

Joseph accepted the indignities and hardships that came, and he eased the experience for his family as he could. After the great adventure of their beginning, the family returned to the home country, and their days settled into the quiet pattern of village life. In the canonical Gospels, only one week during those years bears mentioning, and that only briefly. (The fevered imaginings of the non-canonical gospels have little to no historical value.)

Joseph's son probably received some rudimentary schooling. Even in small villages, Jewish boys had opportunities to learn to read and write, using the Scriptures as their text. Little else is known about such educational programs. We do not know the typical frequency or length of lessons. They were probably conducted in the synagogue, the village's only repository of reading matter. Later Jewish texts recommend that literacy training should begin between the ages of five and seven and end (for most children) before the age of twelve. In a village like Nazareth, the number of school-aged children would have been tiny, perhaps fewer than ten.

---

61   Israel Knohl, *The Messiah before Jesus: The Suffering Servant of the Dead Sea Scrolls* (Berkeley, CA: University of California Press, 2000), 15, 23–24.

In any event, it is clear that Jesus learned his letters, because St. Luke's Gospel depicts him reading aloud from synagogue scrolls (Lk 4:16–20) and St. John shows him writing "with his finger on the ground" (Jn 8:6,8).[62]

By the time his lessons ended, Jesus would already have achieved a degree of independence. He would have grown into a respectable share of his father's work. He would have been gradually eased into adult observance of the religious customs of his people. At age twelve or thirteen, a boy was expected to fulfill all the religious duties of an adult. He would even go to Jerusalem to pay the yearly half-shekel tax at the temple.

For at least seven centuries, every adult male had been required to go to Jerusalem three times a year. The Lord God anticipated this even before the founding of Jerusalem. Moses commanded Israel,

> Three times a year all your males shall appear before
> the LORD your God at the place which he will
> choose: at the feast of unleavened bread, at the feast

62   John P. Meier, *A Marginal Jew: Rethinking the Historical Jesus* (New York: Doubleday, 1991), 271–273. See also Michael Owen Wise, *Language and Literacy in Roman Judaea: A Study of the Bar Kokhba Documents* (New Haven, CT: Yale University Press, 2015), 58–59, 349–350.

of weeks, and at the feast of booths. They shall not appear before the LORD empty-handed. (Dt 16:16)

Only with the construction of the temple by King Solomon was this possible. Only with the reforms of King Josiah was it made mandatory.

The journey was arduous, but it was a joyful duty. Pilgrims thronged the roads, coming to the Holy Land from all corners of the earth. Jews from many nations sang the prescribed Psalms as they approached the city together.

> I was glad when they said to me,
> "Let us go to the house of the LORD!"...
> Jerusalem, built as a city
> which is bound firmly together,
> to which the tribes go up,
> the tribes of the LORD,
> as was decreed for Israel,
> to give thanks to the name of the LORD.
> —Ps 122:1–4

From Nazareth, the journey took four to six days by foot. The caravan would have included some carts and barrows, but most people walked. Each family set out from home with a lamb or goat to offer as sacrifice in the temple on the vigil of the holiday. The procession went forward at the pace of the slowest participants, animal or human.

Women and children had no obligation to make the pilgrimage. The elderly and infirm were exempt. Children, ordinarily, did not go, and their mothers stayed at home to care for them. It was customary, however, in a boy's twelfth year to bring him along to introduce him to the pilgrim's task, which would be his duty in the year that followed.[63]

When Jesus turned twelve, he made the trip with his father. His mother went, too, since there was no one to mind at home.

They went with the pilgrims from their village—and perhaps with others from Kochba, the other village of the House of David. Along the way, they may have encountered old friends or distant relations. Mary was known to have family between Nazareth and Jerusalem. Their caravan was surely a lively, moving crowd by the time they were halfway to the city.

The temple must have been an imposing sight as they drew nearer. It was monumental in size. The Wailing Wall that remains today is sixty feet high—and it was merely the retaining wall at the foot of Herod's masterpiece. The Judean sun at midday reflected brilliantly in the precious gemstones and gold and silver that adorned the temple's towers and parapets.

How lovely is your dwelling place,
O LORD of hosts!

---

63   Joachim Jeremias, *Jerusalem in the Time of Jesus: An Investigation into Economic and Social Conditions during the New Testament Period* (Philadelphia, PA: Fortress, 1969), 76.

My soul longs, yea, faints
for the courts of the LORD;
my heart and flesh sing for joy
to the living God …
For a day in your courts is better
than a thousand elsewhere.
I would rather be a doorkeeper in the house of
    my God
than dwell in the tents of wickedness.
For the LORD God is a sun and shield;
he bestows favor and honor.
—Ps 84:1–2, 10–11

The throng in the roadway would have been impressive to country folk. But it hardly prepared them for the teeming, narrow streets of the city, roaring with the voices of thousands of people.

Jerusalem had undergone "unprecedented colossal development" under Herod the Great and his son Archelaus.[64] Cities at the time were densely crowded as a rule. Experts say that a typical ancient metropolis crammed 160–200 people into an acre. (By way of contrast, American cities in the twenty-first

---

64   Nitza Rosovsky, *City of the Great King: Jerusalem from David to the Present* (Cambridge, MA: Harvard University Press, 1996), 15.

century tend to hold 50–80 people per acre.)[65] Population estimates vary for Jerusalem in the first century, and the range is quite wide. Some place it in the low tens of thousands; others in the mid-hundreds of thousands.[66] Whether the low or high estimates are correct, we know that Jerusalem was a crowded city, and during the pilgrim feasts it was supersaturated; its population more than doubled. Families took in lodgers, as did synagogues. Inns looked forward to the annual spike in business. Still, there were not enough beds in all of Jerusalem for the pilgrims who made the journey. Many stayed in tents just outside the city walls. Others slept in the suburbs and walked to the city for the rites at the temple.[67]

It would make sense for Jesus to accompany his father as they took the family's lamb to the priests for sacrifice. This was his day to acquire the skill as his own—preparing for a time when he might lead the pilgrimage and the *seder* meal himself. Together Jesus and Joseph would have led or carried the lamb to the temple. Together they would have borne the carcass to the courtyards of the city, to be roasted over an open fire.[68] Then together they would have carried the roasted lamb to the place of their *seder*.

---

65   Magen Broshi, *Bread, Wine, Walls and Scrolls* (New York: Sheffield, 2002), 111.

66   Broshi, 110f. See also John Wilkinson, *Jerusalem as Jesus Knew It: Archeology as Evidence* (London: Thames and Hudson, 1978), 23, and Joachim Jeremias, *Jerusalem in the Time of Jesus* (Philadelphia, PA: Fortress, 1969), 77– 84.

67   Jeremias, 61.

68   Wylen, 98.

Since their immediate family was small, their *seder* would have included others—perhaps cousins or neighbors from Nazareth. It was common to extend hospitality also to strangers from faraway places who had no kin in the city. It was normative to have ten people dining at table during the meal.

If Joseph's family was indeed associated with the Essenes, then they might have joined with other likeminded pilgrims. There is evidence that the Essenes met separately for the Passover in their own quarter of the city.[69]

The Passover meal was shared at night by the light of oil lamps, and the most important roles fell to the father and his son.[70] It was probably at this Passover that Joseph led his boy through the traditional rite. God's command to Moses made clear the duty of Joseph and every father: "that you may tell in the hearing of your son ... how I have made sport of the Egyptians and what signs I have done among them; that you may know that I am the LORD" (Ex 10:2).

Placed before the family were the elements of the meal, served in courses: unleavened bread (*matzot*), parsley and salt water, a bitter herb (horseradish or watercress)—and, of

---

69   See Bergsma, 112; also, Bargil Pixner, "Jerusalem's Essene Gateway: Where the Community Lived in Jesus' Time," *Biblical Archaeological Review*, May/June 1997, 23–31, 64–66.

70   For the historical development of the Passover, see Baruch M. Bokser, *The Origins of the Seder: The Passover Rite and Early Rabbinic Judaism* (Berkeley, CA: University of California Press, 1984).

course, the lamb. As the meal proceeded, the father and son recounted the story of Israel's deliverance from Egypt.[71]

The *seder* began with a blessing over wine, the first of four cups of wine to be consumed during the meal. The son would then put questions to his father. He would ask why this night was different from other nights. He would ask the meaning, in turn, of the bitter herbs, the dipping in salt water, the unleavened bread, and the roasted lamb.

The father answered by explaining each food as a sign and memorial of the Exodus. The bread is unleavened because Israel left Egypt in haste—there was no time to let the dough rise. The herbs are bitter to recall the bitterness of slavery. In the course of the father's responses, he would tell the story of Israel's redemption.

The signs were intended to make the moment of the Exodus vividly present and intimately personal for the Chosen People in every age. The rabbis taught: "In every generation a man must regard himself as if he himself came out of Egypt."[72]

Out of Egypt—one wonders, even today, whether that thought brought a smile to the lips of Joseph and Jesus.

The meal moved forward. Joseph broke bread and said a blessing. He pronounced a blessing over the cups of wine.

---

71   Sandmel, 213.
72   *Mishnah Pesachim*, 10.5.

It was typical at a seder in the first century to recite "The Poem of the Four Nights."[73] This brief poem in Aramaic spoke of four events in human history, all of which (according to tradition) took place on the eve of the Passover, the fourteenth day of the Hebrew month Nisan. First was the night of creation, when God made the world out of nothing; second was the night of the *akedah*, when Abraham offered his son Isaac in sacrifice; third was the night of the Exodus, when Israel was liberated from slavery; and the fourth night was still to come. The fourth night was the "night of the messiah," and that too would take place on the fourteenth of Nisan.

At the end of the meal, the family sang six Psalms of praise—Psalms 113–118, known as the Hallel Psalms, followed by Psalm 136, the "Great Hallel."

Jesus would probably return to the young role in future years, and one day he would take on the paternal role, as a rabbi with his disciples.

A father has no idea what his son will make of the lessons of boyhood—the small and large skills passed from one generation to the next. It was Joseph who taught Jesus how to conduct the Passover *seder.* It was Joseph who showed him how to bless the bread and break it—how to bless the cup and share it. It was Joseph who taught him to make thanksgiving by means of the Haggadah, the ancient story of salvation. It

---

73   Andrew Chester, *Divine Revelation and the Divine Titles in the Pentateuchal Targumim* (Tübingen: Mohr, 1986), 193– 94.

was Joseph who read the poem that predicted the night of the messiah.

It was Joseph who gave Jesus the fundamental form that would later come to be filled by the Eucharist.

When the feast was over, the great throng of families and friends re-gathered for the journey to their homelands. They would be joined, perhaps, by others they had met during the festival. The caravans streamed out of the city and onto the wide roads. Friends walked beside companions they might not see for another year or more. Joseph and Mary assumed their son was somewhere in the multitude, with boys his age.

A day into the journey, though, they realized they had not seen him since leaving the city. What began as a twinge of anxiety grew to unbearable sorrow as Joseph and Mary realized their son was nowhere in the caravan—and no one else remembered seeing him since Jerusalem.

They retraced the day's journey, this time at a much quicker pace. Along the way, they made a plan for the sites they would search in the city—the people they might recruit for help.

They knew that the streets would still be crowded with visitors—and not everyone in the city was upright and virtuous. Joseph could have remembered the story of his namesake, the patriarch Joseph, who was taken as a young boy into Egypt. It was a loss that broke the heart of his father, Jacob. It brought a sentence of slavery upon Israel. But it was a pivotal moment in God's plan for his chosen people. Joseph could legitimately have dreaded the pain even as he consciously placed his trust in the Lord.

Day came, and night followed, and day came again; and the couple's sorrow reached the limits of human endurance.

How long, O LORD? Will you forget me forever?
How long will you hide your face from me?
How long must I bear pain in my soul,
and have sorrow in my heart all the day?
—Ps 13:1–2

What joy—what relief—they must have felt, what tears they must have shed, when after three days they found Jesus in the temple. He was sitting among the teachers, listening and asking questions. A crowd was gathered round, astonished by the boy's wisdom (Lk 2:46-47).

Could Joseph—even Joseph the Silent—have seen his son Jesus and not cried out?

It was Mary, though, who spoke:

"Son, why have you treated us so? Behold, your father and I have been looking for you anxiously."
(Lk 2:48)

Jesus addressed both parents: "How is it that you sought me? Did you not know that I must be in my Father's house?" (Lk 2:49).

Any human father would feel pain at those words, and surely Joseph did. It was not a matter of jealousy toward God. Nor was it a matter of wanting credit or gratitude from his son. No, this moment marked a separation that now seemed inevitable. Joseph's boy had become a man. He had reached his maturity, his age of independence, and it was clear that he had a mission to pursue.

Years before, the old man Simeon—right there in the temple—had told Mary that a sword would pierce her heart (Lk 2:35). At this moment, Joseph, too, felt the sword, perhaps as keenly as anything he had felt during yesterday's search.

Joseph and Mary "did not understand the saying" that Jesus spoke to them (Lk 2:50). There is an inevitable incomprehension between generations, and that, too, is a sorrow. Joseph came to feel it, as fathers do.

The family went home, surely changed by the ordeal. Jesus, now grown, willingly submitted to their authority. "He went down with them and came to Nazareth, and was obedient to them" (Lk 2:51).

God himself submitted to Joseph in obedience. What greater testimony to Joseph's righteousness could there be?

CHAPTER 9
A BRIEF REFLECTION ON PRUDENCE

The incident in Jerusalem is history's final glimpse of Joseph. Some of the early Christians held that he lived another seven years before dying what must have been the happiest death possible. He died in the presence of Jesus and Mary. After that, heaven itself could hardly require a transition.

He was a simple man. He chose not to complicate life, but rather keep a singular focus on the objects of his love. With love in mind, all his duties fell into place.

Simplicity is another way that Joseph was godlike. Theologians list simplicity among the characteristics of God. God has no "parts" and no complications. His being is identical to his attributes.

Joseph was a man of integrity in thought and deed. He was loving, provident, generous, and constant. He was an artisan, as God is an artisan. Most importantly, he was Father.

Did he notice the resemblance? Did he notice, furthermore, the similarities that preachers and scholars have seen since the first preaching of the gospel—the similarities between himself and his namesake? The Old Testament Patriarch prefigured the New Testament Father in many ways. Both Josephs received revelations from God in dreams. Both led God's People into Egypt. Both were opposed by mighty powers and faced mortal dangers.

We do not know if Joseph noticed what no Christian can avoid seeing.

When we look at Joseph, we look simultaneously backward in history and forward to completion. The Old Testament types foreshadow a New Testament fulfillment. The New Testament fulfillment, in turn, anticipates a reality that can be comprehended only in eternity.

This side of the veil, Joseph's chief virtue appears to us as prudence.

Prudence is the most misunderstood of the four cardinal virtues. Yet, it is the most important because it is the pre-condition of the other three: justice, temperance, and fortitude. It is prudence that helps a virtuous man steer the middle course of fortitude, for example, between the opposite extremes of cowardice and recklessness.

Prudence is the practical wisdom that enables right action. The *Catechism* defines it as "the virtue that disposes practical reason to discern our true good in every circumstance and to choose the right means of achieving it."[74] St. Thomas Aquinas said that prudence is "right reason in action."[75] It is all about *action*.

And that fact would surely surprise most people today. Prudence is most often presented as *in*action—indecisiveness, irresolution, timidity, extreme caution, constant hesitation. In movies it is often the coward who takes refuge in what he calls "prudence." It is his excuse for hiding or holding back.

The philosopher Joseph Pieper tells us that prudence is the

cause, root, mother, measure, precept, guide, and prototype of all ethical virtues; it acts in all of them, perfecting them to their own nature; all participate in it, and by virtue of this participation they are virtues.[76]

So those who lack prudence also lack all of the other virtues.

---

74   Catechism of the Catholic Church, 2nd ed. (Washington, DC: Libreria Editrice Vaticana–United States Conference of Catholic Bishops, 2000), 1806.

75   Thomas Aquinas, *Summa Theologica*, 2.2.47.3–5.

76   Josef Pieper, *The Four Cardinal Virtues: Human Agency, Intellectual Traditions, and Responsible Knowledge* (Notre Dame, IN: University of Notre Dame Press, 1990), 22.

If Joseph was a just man, it was because he was first a prudent man. If he was a brave man—and he was — it was because he was first a prudent man. Pieper tells us that prudence is the foundation of the structure of the ethical person.

Remember that true prudence is right reason in action. It begins with an apprehension of reality, and it proceeds to actions that correspond to reality. The prudent man makes a habit of seeing the truth—and acting accordingly. It is not enough merely to see it. He must act in consequence.

That is Joseph. There was no Hamlet in him. He was not fainthearted. He did no handwringing. He shunned melodrama. Life was drama enough. Even when Joseph came to the wrong conclusion, he moved forward without fanfare. He "resolved to divorce her quietly." It was his prudence, moreover, that got him out of that jam.

All of the experts say that prudence involves a profound openness to reality. This openness requires humility. Whatever knowledge we have, we have picked up from sensory data, and we know that our senses have limitations. We could be wrong; and that should impose a habitual discipline on what we say or do. We know that reality is not always what it seems to be.

People today find themselves constantly shoulder-deep in data, much of it true, but some of it false to varying degrees. It comes in by way of social media and mainstream outlets, and it is designed not primarily to inform, but rather to provoke, entertain, or exploit those who consume it. It calls for constant prudent discernment. Those who wish to live by St. Thomas's standard will first make sure their reason is right before proceeding to action. They will do as Joseph did.

As a Jew and a son of David, Joseph knew history—especially the history of salvation—so he was able to detect the pattern of God's activity. He knew also how to recognize sin and its consequences. He could judge falsehood because he had steeped himself, all his life, in certain truth: the truth of Sacred Scripture and Tradition.

From Scripture and Tradition, moreover, he knew that he was never alone in any struggle. He knew that he could call upon the help of angels, who were far more powerful than any enemy he might face.

Prudence did not paralyze Joseph. It moved him, instead, to daring action, audacious action, and extreme adventure.

A saint of the twentieth century, St. Josemaría Escrivá, wrote:

> Through prudence, a man learns to be daring
> without being rash. He will not make excuses
> (based on hidden motives of indolence) to avoid the
> effort involved in living wholeheartedly according
> to God's plans. The temperance of the prudent man
> is not insensitive or misanthropic; his justice is not
> harsh nor is his patience servile.[77]

---

77   Josemaría Escrivá, *Friends of God* (New York, NY: Scepter Publishers, 2002), 87.

Prudence can be bold, and often it will be. It is not about false modesty. It does not permit people to say they are less than they actually are, just so that they can excuse themselves from the demands of vocation, family, or career.

Prudence is not a virtue that will make people perennially hold back. It is a fire in their belly to do what they know is right, even though they know it is hard, and even though they would rather not have to do it. Again meditating on Joseph, St. Josemaría said: "We should ask ourselves always: prudence, for what?"[78] Prudence is always oriented to action.

The prudent way—the way of St. Joseph—begins with self-knowledge. People cannot see reality clearly as long as they have those planks in their eyes. They cannot have radical openness to reality if they harbor fears of the truth.

In his discussion of prudence, Pieper warns of something called falsification of memory. He sees this as the great destroyer of the sense of reality. People tend to mythologize their days. They make themselves out to be heroes. They make their adversaries and rivals out to be villains, just because they want the same things. It is hard *not* to see life in this way. But there is no doubt that it is a falsification of memory—and it is corrosive to our sense of reality.

The Christian tradition offers remedies for this. A good spiritual director will not permit his charges to hold on to this kind of thought. He will humanize the rivals they demonize.

---

78   Josemaría Escrivá, *Friends of God,* 85.

Anyone can cultivate that attitude, too, by means of a daily examination of conscience and regular confession. Reality is something that must be faced squarely, deliberately, consciously, with the means God has provided—first, the inner reality of one's self and then the reality of the world.

Joseph can be misunderstood, as prudence is misunderstood. His silence can be mistaken for passivity, but it is not.

Joseph is the prudent man whose thoughts correspond to reality, and whose actions flow from those thoughts. He is the image of God and yet a model for every Christian. He is the one who keeps the constant company of Jesus Christ.

It is good for us, then, to keep company with Joseph. It is good for us to meditate upon his life and find in it a model for our own. This is what tradition calls devotion to St. Joseph.

For almost a millennium, it was neglected so that due honor might be paid to Joseph's immaculate spouse, the Blessed Virgin Mary. In the second millennium, however, the Church turned increasingly to the carpenter from Nazareth—with the way illumined by St. Bernard of Clairvaux, St. Thomas Aquinas, St. Bernardine of Siena, St. Francis de Sales, and St. Teresa of Avila. Modern scholars argue persuasively that devotion to St. Joseph came to full flourishing with the discovery of the Americas—in French Canada and

Spanish America. Nowhere is the saint portrayed as beautifully as in the seventeenth- and eighteenth-century paintings of the Cuzco School (*Escuela Cuzqueña*). Nowhere is he honored so monumentally as at the Oratory of St. Joseph in Montreal, Quebec.[79]

The saints of the second millennium were fond of invoking the words of the good Pharaoh, in the Book of Genesis. When all the land was famished he told his people: "*Go to Joseph*; what he says to you, do" (Gn 41:55).

What was foreshadowed in the Old Testament is fulfilled in the New. What Joseph of Nazareth "says" to us today, he says through his prudent actions. He speaks through his deeds, which we know from the Gospels.

The saints of the second millennium were also fond of reminding us that Jesus chose to be obedient to his father Joseph (Lk 2:51)—and it is unlikely he has given up that good habit, even today. What Joseph asks of his son, his son is quick to accomplish, whether it is the planing of a plank or the grace of courage for a soul in distress.

In many ways, our world is different from Joseph's. The craft of carpentry, for example, is enhanced by remarkable machinery. The journey from Palestine to Egypt can

---

79   For the history of devotion to St Joseph, see Joseph F. Chorpenning, ed., *Joseph of Nazareth through the Centuries* (Philadelphia, PA: St. Joseph's University Press, 2011). See also Joseph F. Chorpenning, ed., *Patron Saint of the New World: Spanish American Colonial Images of St. Joseph* (Philadelphia, PA: St. Joseph's University Press, 1992), 1.

be completed in less than a day, assuming one has the right passport.

But the world still runs on the same principles. Human nature has not changed over the millennia. We face the same moral challenges as ever. We find stunning beauty in all the same places: the far horizon, the nearest faces, the sweep of mountains and valleys, and the music and truth of a few lines from a poem.

We travel our world more confidently when we know the story of Joseph in his world. We will reach our destination more surely if we have Joseph as our companion.